YOU CAN...
WRITE YOUR BOOK
IN A WEEKEND

SECRETS BEHIND THIS PROVEN,
LIFE-CHANGING, TRULY UNIQUE,
INSIDE-OUT APPROACH

TOM BIRD

You Can... Write Your Book in a Weekend

Copyright © 2013 by Tom Bird

For permissions:

Sojourn Publishing, LLC, 280 Foothills South Dr., Sedona, AZ 86336

ISBN-13: 978-1-62747-007-0 (paperback)
ISBN-13: 978-1-62747-008-7 (ebook)

Printed in the United States of America

CONTENTS

DEDICATION

To Skyla, who has always brought a love so deep into my life that I never knew existed. It is from this love that I now see in everything around me. It is this love that I no longer choose to live without.

INTRODUCTION

"It was the best of times, it was the worst of times."

THERE ARE MANY WAYS TO REACH A DIRECT communicative connection with the being who goes by many names and who is most commonly referred to as God.

Jack Nicholson has captivated the world on so many occasions with his provocative performances as a variety of characters in a variety of movies, each time offering every one of us an enhanced understanding and thus changing our lives. Michael Jordan did so while "in the Zone" on the basketball court. President John F. Kennedy and civil rights leader Martin Luther King Jr. did so while speaking. African American communities did it almost on a daily basis, singing their gospel hymns while toiling in the oppressively hot cotton fields. Eckhart Tolle did so while sitting silently, in a receptive mood, on the same park bench at the same time each day.

Each one of the aforementioned persons connected directly with God and in doing so changed the world.

"An atheist is a man who has no invisible means of support."

—JOHN BUCHAN

As this book will show, you can do the same through writing your book. Not only will you change the world but you will change every aspect of your own personal world for the better. The earlier quote was written by Charles Dickens in his classic *A Tale of Two Cities*. In his book Dickens was describing another time and another age. Or was he?

"It was the best of times, it was the worst of times, it was the age of wisdom, it was the age of foolishness, it was the epoch of belief, it was the epoch of incredulity..."

Our economy has crumbled. As we attempt to rebuild it we are being forced to do so from a completely different perspective. No longer does the conscious, dog-eat-dog, win-at-all-costs, it's-just-business approach to a vocation seem to work. Everything seems to have gone in a different direction—with which we are struggling to keep pace.

That direction is reflective solely of treating each other well, looking out for our neighbors, colleagues, bosses, employees, friends, and families, and completely coming from the heart with what it is you do with your life.

> "God is subtle, but He is not malicious."
>
> —ALBERT EINSTEIN

Maybe it could have been, should have been, that way all along. Nonetheless, it is that way now, and it appears as though we are being forced to move in that direction or continue to perish.

> "...it was the season of Light, it was the season of Darkness, it was the spring of hope, it was the winter of despair..."

Sure, the unemployment rate hasn't been this high since the Great Depression, but maybe with so many jobs tied to careers and incomes that do not speak of our higher purpose, maybe that jobless rate needs to be as high as it is. Maybe life—the Creator, the universe, the soul itself—is calling for us to make a necessary shift to a complete heart-based lifestyle. Maybe it is forcing us to do that right now, before we destroy ourselves and the planet on which we live.

"Many of life's failures are people who did not realize how close they were to success when they gave up."

—THOMAS EDISON

"…we had everything before us, we had nothing before us, we were all going direct to heaven, we were all going direct the other way."

What do your reading of this book and your writing have to do with all of that? First, you may or may not be aware of an article that was published in *The New York Times* a few years ago. The article cited a survey that claimed 81 percent of Americans felt they had a book stuck inside them that they had to get out. Based on our most recent census, 81 percent of Americans would equate to nearly a quarter of a billion people. If we assumed that the same percentage of persons was worldwide, that would be close to 4.8 billion people. Are there possibly that many would-be authors out there?

"Many suffer from the incurable disease of writing, and it becomes chronic in their sick minds."

—JUVENAL

Yes and no. No, because it would be impossible to believe that so many people, with all of the potential professions out there, would be drawn to one specific vocation. Yes, because it is very possible that the writing of a book may carry more with it than just the promise of a vocation.

In fact, Aristotle believed that to live a full and complete life a person needed to do three things: 1) build a home; 2) raise a child; and 3) write a book.

Yes, that's correct, write a book. It was the great Aristotle who believed that writing a book was one of the three absolutely necessary pillars of life. Based upon my nearly three decades of working with tens of thousands of aspiring authors worldwide, I wholeheartedly agree.

In-depth experience has illustrated much for me. It has shown me that *every* person has a book inside them.

How do I know this? I know this because I have not befriended anyone, at one level or another, who has not wanted to write a book at one time or another in their lives. Sure, some of those people only felt that they had a book in them for six minutes after swallowing a six-pack of beer, while others held onto the dream for decades. Nonetheless, at one time or another— no matter how short that "another" may have been— everyone, at some point in his or her life, wants to write a book.

Why? The second thing that the experience has taught me is that when applying a "natural," as opposed to a consciously contrived approach to writing the book a would-be author feels is inside, an amazing transformation can be witnessed in every area of life.

Whether or not they are directly connecting with a divine presence outside themselves or connecting with that presence already available within each one of us is a topic for another book. Either way, that connection is definitely made through the writing of their books and their lives change for the better as a result.

> "You have to leave the city of your comfort and go into the wilderness of your intuition.
>
> What you'll discover will be wonderful. What you'll discover is yourself."
>
> —ALAN ALDA

As that connection is made, especially over the length of time it takes to write a book, the author heals relationships, rights wrongs, cleanses wounds, finds purpose, releases divine voices, births and reinvigorates new vocations that had become stagnant and in general, lives a better life.

> "In the depth of winter, I finally learned that within me there lay an invincible summer."
>
> —ALBERT CAMUS

Am I saying that the type of divine experience I am describing is only possible through the writing of a book? No, I am not saying that. However, what I am saying is that there is something divinely unique, beautiful, marvelous, and mysterious released directly into the lives of individuals through the authoring of books the "natural" way.

> "Resolve to be thyself; and know that he who finds himself, loses his misery."
>
> —MATTHEW ARNOLD

"The innate human need that underlies all writing, the need to give shape to your experience, is a gift we all possess from earliest childhood," states Gabriele Rico in her bestselling book *Writing the Natural Way*.

This is evidenced by the fact that persons who have obviously reached some type of divine connection still gravitate toward writing a book. In many cases—I may be preaching to the choir here—people often feel so drawn to writing a book that deep down inside they realize their lives will not be complete unless they get out whatever story is inside them. However, very rarely does that work in the reverse. Very rarely do people who, after they become successful authors, suddenly want to transfer their energies to dancing, singing, sports, acting, or politics, for example. No, there is just something special about writing.

> "I did not write it. God wrote it. I merely did His dictation."
>
> —HARRIET BEECHER STOWE

That something, which is so one-of-a-kind-special, has led me to believe that everyone should write a book at some point in their lives. The earlier the better, if not for the vocational opportunities available then for the unmatched, can't-seem-to-get-anywhere-else alternatives that are available from doing so. I am not alone in that belief. America's most famous and well-respected family, the Kennedys, have long understood and believed in the power, possibility, and release associated with the writing of a book. Just look at how many books they have written. They have encouraged their children, from JFK Jr. to Bobby Kennedy Jr., to write. Could writing have led the children, those famous Kennedys, to their great, oftentimes earth-changing, lives? No one can say for sure, for there may not be an absolute way of measuring a correlation between writing a book and living a successful life.

Just look what a bestseller, *The Hurricane* by Rubin "Hurricane" Carter, did for the author. How about Nelson Mandela and Solzhenitsyn, who wrote their earth-shaking books while in prison as well? Writing their books in prison led to their freedom from that prison emotionally, spiritually and oftentimes physically as well. What they wrote about or experienced while in their prison cells led to their fame and fortune, through the release of their message, once they were set free.

Could what these moving authors experienced be analogies to what all of us have faced in our lives or are facing right now? Could it be that we are all in some sort of self-imposed prison, some more obvious than others, until we write our books? Could it be that those prisons in which we find ourselves are there specifically to encourage the writing of our books?

Could that lack of a job or purpose in your life right now create some sort of prison for you as well, where you feel especially locked up with a lot of time on your hands to do....nothing? Maybe it is, as Tolle would view it, that nothingness which needs to be filled, longs to be filled, with the writing of a book. If everything does happen for a reason, could the reason that you may have a lot of time on your hands or seek to have a lot of time on your hands have to do with the fact that the prison which you have created for yourself has appeared to lead you to writing your book?

It is said that a great book changes the lives of many. I believe that the greatest change experienced by writing a book is for the author doing the writing. In fact, despite all of the money and fame that can be earned by doing so, if that were not the case no one would ever make it through the penning of a book. Doing so is just too hard and the motivation not great enough.

There is an off-balance belief in unsuccessful writing circles that you should always write to your audience. What they mean is that you should write co-dependently to the needs of those you want to like your work, those who will buy your books. Nothing could be farther from the truth. Sure, you should write for your audience. On that point I agree. However, the audience that you should write for is the audience of yourself. For then and only then can you successfully acknowledge and appreciate and thus grow, change, and heal from the experience of writing.

Could adhering to inappropriately designed, truly unexplored sayings and beliefs such as the one above, be the reason that the writing of a book has become so difficult, if not impossible, by the well-meaning, hardworking, impassioned souls of our planet?

Yes. In fact, as you will see in the story that follows, I encountered nothing but failure when investing in the "orthodox" approaches to writing, and it was only when I totally began adhering to the complete opposite of what I had been told or taught that I began to experience the success that I deserved as an author.

Such has been the case with, I would venture to say, every person that has ever entered one of my classes or workshops. In one way or another, each person is a writing refugee. Each has tried, on one level or another, to "birth" a book only to be met with frustration and failure. Could it be that what they had learned about writing up until that point had been the cause?

Yes. In fact, once they blend with the method I have used to experience my own success, the one which I teach, then and only then do they transition. Once they transition, all of a sudden writing becomes easy and joyful once again, just like they experienced so long ago before someone "taught" them how to write, as opposed to showing them how to potentially unbridle and release themselves to write.

You see, I don't teach them how to write. I simply help them reconnect with the authors they already are, beyond all that they learned. Once there, all they had lost suddenly returns, they birth their books in record times, and they change their own lives— for their audiences and for themselves.

Everyone should write a book because everyone is meant to write a book. It is the sole way of delivering the message we were all born to live and then leave behind, first to the author himself or herself and then to the outside audience. It is from that perspective, and from what feels like several lifetimes of experience in this area, that this book is written.

"… in short, the period was so far like the present period, that some of its noisiest authorities insisted on its being received, for good or for evil, in the superlative degree of comparison only."

—CHARLES DICKENS

A Tale of Two Cities

Perhaps it has become obvious that you do need to make a career shift. Perhaps it has become obvious that your career needs to be invigorated in a big way, and the presence of a book authored by you, in your particular area of interest, would more than help. Perhaps there is a greater calling inside you. You can just feel it, but don't know how to get to it. Writing a book can get you there. Maybe you have finally just gotten tired of trying to outrun all of the pain, anger, and frustration that has dogged you for what feels like forever. Perhaps you need a route to release it (the subject of many a great book) in order to heal those parts of you. Perhaps you need to be offered another perspective, a lifesaving one, before it is too late. Perhaps all of the above descriptions apply to you. Perhaps only one or two of them. Either way, it's time to write your book.

Now, before we go any further and your logical "can't do it, can't even try" mindset gets a hold of this concept, I need to clarify something. I'm not talking about the resurrection of your life, career, and relationships taking the rest of your years on this planet. I'm talking about getting all of this done in three days—three short days—to change your life. You can change your outlook on relationships (especially the one with yourself), health, vocation, your total perspective of your time here on this planet, and much more in three days. Three Days! Not several decades or centuries.

Look at this realistically. What would you invest to accomplish that which you can derive from writing? You may have already invested tens of thousands, if not hundreds of thousands of dollars in a college or university education, not to mention all those years, and you are still reading this book. How many of the tens of thousands of English or journalism majors walk out after graduation with either a bachelor's or master's degree or a Ph.D. and yet have not written the publishable book: the real reason they entered into the program they chose in the first place?

Since the results I am seeking would be so dismally depressing, I don't want to go there completely.

However, I would say over 98 percent would be a reasonable guesstimate. Then what do so many of these people, as driven and as intelligent and committed as they are, end up directing all of their talents toward? Teaching. Correct. Then from their positions as teachers, they do what? Share everything they know about writing, despite the fact that they have yet to become, or even remotely experience the personal/professional success that they themselves could seek as authors.

"Our loss begins in school, when the process of writing is taught to us in fragments: mechanics, grammar, and vocabulary," says Gabriele Rico in her book *Writing the NaturalWay*. "Writing becomes fearful and loathsome, a workbook activity. Students write as little as possible, and once out of school, they tend to avoid the entire process whenever possible. As a result, few people turn to writing as a natural source of pleasure and gratification.

"This is sad because children's writing naturally has an expressive position, an authenticity that inherently captures the sound of an individual on a page, an ability we seem to lose the more we learn about writing."

> "When we were little we had no difficulty sounding the way we felt; thus, most little children speak and write with real voice."
>
> —PETER ELBOW
>
> *Writing with Power*

"Most of the methods of training the conscious side of the writer—the craftsman and the critic inside of him—are actually hostile to the good of the artist's side," says Dorothea Brande in her book, *Becoming a Writer*.

"A lot of people in English departments should never be trusted to run a program," says legendary author Wallace Stegner. "Their training is all in the other direction, all analytical, all critical. It's all reader's training, not a writer's training, so they have no notion of how to approach the opportunity."

Collectively, how many years and how much money on average did they invest in accomplishing the completion of a program that personally left them high and dry as the author they really wanted to become? Have you taken a look at results from standardized test scores for high school students lately? With everything else that is going on in our society, you may not want to if you have already had enough depressing news for now.

> "This is the sort of English up with which I will not put."

> —WINSTON CHURCHILL

One of the darkest holes in our educational system is directly tied to how much money our federal government devotes to re-educating teachers on their ability to improve their skills in teaching students to write. Does this tell you something? It does to me. That's the bad news; now back to the good news.

> "He must forget the things he does not wish to remember and remember only the things he wishes to retain."

—BAIRD T. SPALDING

Life and Teaching of the Masters of The Far East

You can have your literary dream, no matter what motivates you toward living it, right here and right now. You don't need any previous 'qualifications'. In fact, the few you *do* have, the better because there will be less relearning for you to do. You can accomplish this release and rebirthing of your deepest spiritual, expressive self, which was jammed into its own unlivable space so long ago. You can live your literary dream, if that is what you seek to do, in less than a week.

The method behind my Write Your Publishable Book in a Weekend retreats leads over 98 percent of those involved, who are of all ages and come from all walks of life and educational levels, to the completion of their books in that period of time. In fact, the only ones who attend the retreats and normally don't complete their books in that period of time are those who, for whatever reason, miss a day or two of the retreat. It isn't that the method doesn't work for them. It's just that they simply run out of time before completing their books.

"The potential for natural writing is already within all of us; it is not too late for any of us to learn," states Rico.

However, again (and this is worth repeating), it is possible to actually become the author you want to be while also experiencing firsthand all the life-changing aspects of writing a book right now in a weekend, for a price equivalent to one fifth of the average cost of a semester's tuition at a middle-of-the-road college or university. How much have you already invested in a career, vocation, or psychotherapy?

Sorry, but I can't help you do anything about what you have already invested. All I can help you with is moving forward, right now, through writing a book and experiencing all the wondrous gifts and opportunities it presents. All you will need to experience them, the vast array of them, is a long weekend.

These questions would be more appropriate to ask yourself instead. What would it be worth to you to be able to birth your deepest, most purpose-connected self? How would that change your life? How would that change the lives of those around you? How would that change the world?

Take a moment to ponder those questions again once more before reading on.

We're not talking three, around-the-clock days. When done properly, as described in this book, we're talking about three, eight-hour days—kind of like going to work at a normal job for a long weekend. In that short amount of time you will learn all that you need to carry you through the rest of your life. All that has held you back to this point from being able to write will surface and be released. All that lies before you as a soul will be laid out in front of you, like a newly paved autobahn constructed just for you and only you. It will be your road, your path, the one you were meant to drive down solely, at whatever speed or rate you prefer to travel.

Can writing a book really do that for you? Yes. So as not to bore you with written testimonial after testimonial here, if you haven't already done so, I would suggest that you visit my website *www.TomBird.com*. There you will find dozens of video testimonials from budding authors of all ages and from all walks of life.

What you will find there will inspire you and possibly even stun you. You will hear a part of yourself, a universal part of us all, speaking directly to you through not only what you hear the retreat attendees say, but from where they share it—a place in all of us, as well.

What do you need for this journey you are about to embark upon? Besides the heart, which is an author's most important ingredient, and the place from where all great books express themselves, what is it that you should bring to the table beside the obvious, including a computer?

- **First,** even though some of you will be using your keyboards to pen your books, all of you will still be doing some necessary writing in longhand, so **a nice writing utensil or two would be great.** By nice, I mean one that fits your hand well and moves smoothly across a piece of paper. Nice does not always translate into "expensive." The cheaper versions of pens are oftentimes just as good, if not better, than high-priced ones. The main aspects to keep in mind when acquiring the right writing utensil(s) are simply how well a pen fits your hand, how much ink gets to its ball, and how quickly, as a result, it can thus move across the page.

- **Second**, you will need paper. Yes, as I mentioned before (just stay with me here— it will all be okay, I promise), you will at times be using a pen to write on paper. Initially, this is how you will be asked to approach the writing of your book, instead of through your beloved computer. Don't worry though, you will receive the opportunity to transfer your efforts to the keyboard, which you have come to know and love so well. There will be more on this later. What I suggest is that you purchase one 14" x 17" drawing pad, one regular-sized lined note pad, and a small lined note pad.

- **Third,** go to my website *www.TomBird.com*. On the site you will see a tab entitled "Free." Click on that tab. Scroll down until you find the link that allows you to download a copy of my relaxation/subliminal CD, *Transitioning Back to the Writer You Were Meant* *to Be*. You will be using this CD liberally as you glide your way through your book. It will become the sail that catches and directs back to you the wind of inspiration that will serve as your guide to reconnect with all that really matters in your life. Or, if you have purchased the cyber version of this book, you can access that simply by clicking right here. So important is the use of this CD that I would recommend playing both the first track, which is only a few minutes long, then the second while reading this book or doing any writing of any kind.

"In order to achieve great things, we must live as though we were never going to die."

—MARQUIS DE VAUVENARGUES

- **Finally**, you will need time, far less time than you may believe—three days to be exact— after reading this book.

"He who rides a tiger is afraid to dismount."

—PROVERB

Do you want to know about me, my story, and how I came to the revelations that changed my life? Continue reading.

Chapter One

Tom's Tale

I FEEL THAT IF YOU ARE GOING TO PONY UP TO THE TABLE with your time and energy, not to mention your intestinal fortitude, the very least I can do is share a bit more with you about who I am and where the plan you will be following came from. Plus, I have found that there are just so many less-than-worthy-folks out there, hiding in the shadows, talking about writing and especially spirituality, that you at least deserve to know a little bit about me, my method, and how I came to pen this book. So, here's my story.

* * * *

Late one summer evening, at the age of fourteen, as I lay on my parents' side lawn staring up at the stars, I asked the question that had haunted me for years.

"Why is it that I want to write?"

I was asking the One who goes by many names but is most often referred to as God. I had always had a good, close, personal relationship with God. Thank God (no pun intended). I was just coming to grips with the fact that my childhood had been much more difficult on me than I realized, and it was to God I ran each day to talk and listen. So by my mid-teens, having a heart-to-heart with the Almighty had become rather routine. I knew I would receive an answer to my question. As it came back I could feel my body vibrating with every word as it formed. It was almost as if God had been waiting for me to ask this very question and it was as though I could actually feel God's excitement coming through with the reply.

"You want to write, you were born to write because you see so much beauty and wonder in the world and this is the best way to convey it so others can begin to see it and enjoy it as well," the voice said, straightforward, direct, and clear.

Finally, the obsession I had since childhood finally began to make sense; reason began to appear behind my obsession, this urge to write which began at the age of eight.

> "It is not necessary to seek God because God is already the essence of who you are. To connect with God, simply remove all judgments and thoughts that do not bless you and others."
>
> —PAUL FERRINI

The answer came through so crisply and clearly. I wondered why I had waited so long to ask the question in the first place. My delay must have had to do with my feeling of unworthiness. I mean, who was I, the son of a blue-collar father, to think that someone would actually want to read what I had to say? Who was I to even think I had the ability to write well enough for people to want to read what I wrote as well?

> "What is a weed? A plant whose virtues have not yet been discovered."
>
> —RALPH WALDO EMERSON

Looking back now though, all the signs were there. All that was off was the attitude I had toward myself. Recognition of what I was meant to do with my life vocationally first came to me at the age of eight. That year for Christmas, my aunt and uncle had given me a two-foot-by-three-foot cork bulletin board. Immediately after hanging it in my bedroom, a never-ending stream of words began pouring through me and I began writing them down and tacking them up on the board.

In no time at all, the corkboard was completely full. I began using the tacks to hold more than one scrap of paper. Soon the tacks would hold no more, and I began capturing my inspirations in notebooks. It was at that time I realized that deep down inside I was a writer.

From that time forward, writing always came easily for me. In fact, I finished in the top two percentile nationally in communication skills on my college placement exams, this after I had literally refused to participate in any form of writing and/or studying in high school.

Another time while in college, I was assigned to write a review on a play for my college newspaper. However, I only had twenty-five minutes to complete the review after the play was done to be able to get the article in on time. Of course, the short amount of time I would have to complete the piece would not allow me to do any "thinking" (much more on this later).

I finished the piece in fifteen minutes. I received more compliments on my writing from that piece than I had received from all the other articles I had written previously for the paper combined.

My theory about the naturalness of writing being

available to all of us, almost like it was a God-given gift bestowed upon all of us, was taking shape.

> "We do not write in order to be understood;
> we write in order to understand."
>
> —C. DAY LEWIS

Shortly after graduating from college, I moved on to a one-season temporary internship with the Pittsburgh Pirates and for the first time in my life I felt pressure to become like everyone else.

I had only taken the job with the Pirates because of my love for baseball, which was second only to how deeply I felt about writing. I had possibly been the only senior on campus that hadn't applied for any jobs. I didn't want a job. I wanted to write, to be an author. I hadn't ever been clearer on anything in my young life.

Despite my academic complacency in high school, I transformed myself into an outstanding student at the university level. My college, in an effort to further its reputation, fixed me up with the Pirates. That year was 1979, the magical season of Willie "Pops" Stargell and the "Family," the most charismatic group of ballplayers in the modern era of baseball. The Pirates won the World Series that season. Pops brought us back from a three-games-to-one deficit to win a deciding Game Seven with a classic homerun. He had promised to hit that homerun only a few hours earlier for an eleven-year-old boy dying of leukemia who openly realized he would not make it through that night.

As exciting as the season had been, I never had any aspirations to stay with the Pirates. With the World Series every kid had always wanted to win under my belt, I was planning to follow my heart to New York, where I was going to settle in and write my first book. However, I had become a fixture with the Family. I was offered a big raise and a permanent position was established just for me, so I allowed myself to be convinced to stay.

Yet the writer in me kept calling to be let out. It relentlessly drove me to use whatever few free hours I had to feverishly follow the callings of my heart.

> "Surrender does not transform what is, at least not directly.
>
> Surrender transforms you. When you are transformed, your whole
>
> world is transformed because the world is only a reflection."

> —ECKHART TOLLE
>
> *The Power of Now*

However, by that time, practicality had set its roots deeply within me. For the first time, I thought I had to be an authority on writing and publishing to become the author I longed to be. As a result, I forgot all about my theory on the naturalness of writing.

By that time I recognized that my college education hadn't been able to offer me the evolution as an author that I had sought. So, I took to reading every book on writing that I could find. In eighteen months I had read them all, filling 148 legal pads with notes. In those pads, I was sure the conscious, magic formula I longed for would be found, but what I sought couldn't be found there.

I then turned to the biggest asset that I had at that time: my job with the Pirates, which put me in the company of many bestselling and world-renowned authors. Liberally utilizing my extensive contacts, I began interviewing every author I could. To each one I asked the same question, "How do you become an author?"

The best answer I got was from Dick Young, the so-called Dean of American Sports Writers at the time, who replied to my question by simply saying, "You write."

I initially poo-pooed Dick's response, not realizing its true significance. I kept going solely because I did not believe that God would have given me such a strong calling to write without providing me with the route to live it; of that, more than anything else in my life, I was sure. Yet, on the other hand, I was still convinced that I had to find the necessary formula that so many hundreds of thousands, if not millions, had sought before me on not only how to easily and enjoyably write books but get them published as well. However, it was nowhere to be found, neither in all the obvious places I looked, nor within all the orthodox methods I had studied. They were a deep and dark frustration at the time.

It is my firm belief that many of us don't change until the pain becomes so great that we have to. As a result, desperation can be a necessary predecessor to greatness, and at that time in my life I was feeling very desperate.

Finally, tired of feeling this pain and not being able to find any solution, I got down on my knees and asked for divine guidance. I expressed my frustration. I shared the fears that I had about living my life without being able to live my dream, and how I felt that doing so was really dying. Then I realized the true reason for my despair. The despair had to do with the fact that I had stopped writing, which had come so naturally to me, and as a result I had severed my truest and most direct connection with God. It was also at that time that I promised to share with others whatever solutions God would offer me so that they, hopefully, wouldn't have to suffer as long or as hard as I had been suffering.

Two mornings later I woke up hours before my alarm was set to go off, and I heard the words of Dick Young rolling around over and over again in my head. It was then that I finally realized that when I had started searching, I had stopped writing, which was the very reason my connection with God had been severed and my life had become such a depressing mess shortly thereafter.

> "Unprovided with original learning, unformed in the habits of thinking, unskilled in the arts of composition, I resolved to write a book."

—EDWARD GIBBON

So, I returned to what had once come so naturally for me. In response, the words literally seemed to write themselves. In fact, I felt stronger and more jazzed after writing the 4,000 or so words than I did at any other time during the day. I could see a clearer and deeper meaning behind everything that was happening in my life. I knew exactly what it was that I needed to do: write, write, and continue to write daily, every hour, every minute of my time that I could squeeze out.

Embedded in the act of actually writing, what most writers miss, is the faith, the wisdom, and the direction one needs to live life. I also clearly understood that I didn't have to try to be something I had been since I was born. I had already connected with my inner author, which I now refer to as my Divine Author Within (DAW), my true and absolute pipeline to the natural communicative abilities between God and every one of us, which I had left behind when I tried to figure out how to become what I already was.

"Literary men are. . .a perpetual priesthood."

—THOMAS CARLYLE

As a result of that realization, amazing things began happening in my life. Overnight my DAW urged me to approach Willie, the most popular athlete in the country at the time, about co-authoring his life story.

However, no matter how strong the draw was, I was deeply hesitant. Willie Stargell had been severely taken advantage of by a co-author a few years earlier. This author had chosen to fabricate certain aspects of Willie's story to make it a more sensational read. Since opting out of the deal, Willie had sworn never to become embroiled in a project like that one again. However, after working together through one World Series victory and the Pirates' next three seasons, Willie and I were the best of friends. I was hesitant to approach him, though, since I didn't in any way want to jeopardize our friendship.

Nonetheless, the draw to speak with him wouldn't let me go. I finally approached him and confessed my aspirations. Willie listened attentively and compassionately, as he always did. He then shared his reflections of the pain, frustration, and embarrassment he, his friends, and his family had suffered at the hands of his former co-author. Yet, he concluded by telling me that there was one and only one person with whom he would ever trust enough to enter into a venture of that sort again...and I was that person.

The incident caused me to see how my purpose, my dream of becoming an author, and most of all my connection, had never given up on me, even though I had tried to give up on them. They were willing to follow me wherever I strayed.

Never having sold a book before, I once again asked for divine guidance. Shortly after arriving in my office the following morning, the man who ran our mailroom came in with my morning's stack of mail. In it was a brochure from Scott Meredith, a literary agent in New York; how he had gotten my address I did not know. Nor did I know at the time that Scott was the top literary representative in the world.

So, unknowingly, I casually picked up the phone and gave him a call. After I explained why I was phoning, his receptionist quickly patched me through. Once Scott heard what I had to say, he couldn't wait to meet with Willie and I. Coincidentally, the team was scheduled to be in Manhattan the following week to play the New York Mets, so a meeting was planned.

> "No matter where your life takes you, no matter how far you stray from the path, you cannot
>
> extinguish the spark of divinity within your own consciousness.
>
> It was and is God's gift to you."
>
> —PAUL FERRINI

Once the three of us got together, an immediate kinship formed. Scott gave us both his private home phone number, signed us to a contract, and we were on our way.

Six weeks after that date, Scott sold my first book to Harper & Row, the third largest publisher in the world, and Larry Ashmead, one of the business's finest editors. Scott sold it for an amount equivalent to three times my yearly salary.

All of this transpired less than two months after I directly reconnected back with my DAW, and thus, with God. Since then, I have discovered through my students that this kind of miraculous event is not atypical.

However, as wonderful as my first book's sale happened to be, I found myself faced with the daunting dilemma of having to author a book, and I had no logistical idea how to go about doing so. Yet there was one thing that I had become very good at over the last few months, and that was reconnecting with my DAW and listening to God.

I was still working with the Pirates when I began my first book, which meant I was still responsible for working seven days a week for an average of fifteen hours a day. To accommodate my commitment, I got up two hours earlier each morning to write. This simple routine enabled me to complete a manuscript within six months that brought Willie to tears, and which our editor praised as a strong literary work.

It was my second book, though, that allowed me to perfect and understand what I had done so spontaneously with my first work. I was living in a bustling suburb of Pittsburgh at the time. Pittsburgh has a reputation for many things. For those of us who have lived there, the traffic jams created by its many tunnels and bridges were one of the worst.

I make no bones about it: I despise traffic. I realize

that no one likes it, but because I dislike traffic so much more than most, I am willing to do literally anything I can to avoid it. As bad as the traffic is in Pittsburgh during weekday rush hours, it was nearly as bad on the weekends when most people were off work.

So, entering into my second book, I made the decision to test what I had learned by writing only on the weekends, when the traffic in my neighborhood usually came to a standstill. My thinking was that not only would I be able to avoid the traffic I disliked so much, but I would also be able to evaluate what I thought I learned from my first book.

By then I had come to theorize that the reason a person wanted to write had nothing to do with the actual act of writing itself. Instead, a person sought to write because he or she had a divine message in the form of a book—signed, sealed, and delivered inside them—that was trying to get out. The statistic I quoted in the introduction from the article in *The New York Times* attests to that fact.

My tested and well-founded belief also led me to theorize that, because of this divine connection, we should be able to relay these already finished works onto paper in about the same amount of time that it would take us to literally copy down that book.

If my theory was correct, I would be able to capture the entire 80,000-word draft of my second book in twelve days or less, and then revise and perfect that draft in three days or less. My final calculations for how long it would take from start to finish would add up to fifteen days, or five three-day weekends.

Much to my delight, creating the formal timeline calmed the concerns and fears of my logical mind, and as a result I was able to give in to the process even more deeply and easily.

Right from the beginning of writing book two, I could tell that I was on to something brilliant. The words began flowing out of me like water spraying from a hose. Even more important was the fact that I loved the way I felt when I wrote. I looked forward so much to writing that I became positively addicted to it.

I zoomed through the writing and revision of my second book, from the first word to the last, in the five consecutive three-day weekends I had allotted. To be able to reach that stage with my book in that short amount of time was an unfathomable high. Little did I know that I would eventually be called to lead other authors to do it as well. I was still reeling from the effects of my excitement as I slipped my manuscript into the mail to the publisher.

However, stagnant time for a writer is the mother of all self-doubt. Sitting idle can cause a mountain of problems, as your mind and all of its worries and fears finally catch back up with you. That is exactly what happened in my case. In a mere few days, my opinion of the experience had completely changed, and I was more than sure I had just made the biggest mistake of my young literary life.

Ten days after I had mailed in the manuscript I could no longer control myself, so I called my publisher searching for some sort of validation.

To my surprise he not only loved the book, but found so few mistakes that he didn't feel any sort of rewriting was necessary. So, I chose to employ the exact same methods with my third book, which I had been given five months to write. My publisher, Zondervan, was deeply concerned that the deadline was too tight, so I believe that they gave me a larger-than-average advance to compensate for my inconvenience.

I completed that book in a month and a half, but waited the remainder of the five months before I turned it in. I just didn't want to disillusion them. A favorable response was received from them as well.

True to my word, soon after the completion of book one, I began following through on my promise to God to share what I had learned with other aspiring writers. In no time at all, word of my work spread through the local and then national writing communities. Over the next thirty-one years, I gleefully divided my time between writing my next books and making over 4,000 appearances at over 100 colleges and universities.

Then, while standing in front of a packed classroom at the University of Arizona in January 2000, my next revelation came to me as I was overcome with the strangest of feelings. I recognized it as my own DAW coming through.

By that time, I had learned the value of always following the advice of my DAW, which on this occasion was nudging me to steer those in attendance to begin writing their books right then and there, without any of the necessary preparatory steps I had employed in the past.

Shortly after, I upgraded my system to directly emulate what I learned could be done that day. Once I implemented the system with my students I began seeing even more clearly the potential of this ultimate connection, as aspiring writers from all ages, beliefs, and backgrounds composed more than 10,000 words per day and completed books and screenplays in as little as two or three weeks.

In fact, the first fifty students with whom I chose to share this program completed over 100 books in one year with no compromises in quality. More importantly, their lives transformed as their biases and fears were removed and replaced by the fulfillment of their dreams and the recognition of their life purpose.

Of course, that is just the beginning of my tale. For later on, further inspirations led me to create the Write Your Book in 90 Days, and then forty-five days, and then thirty days, and then Write Your Book in 8 Days retreat, then the Write Your Book in 5 Days retreat, and then the Write Your Publishable Book in a Weekend retreat.

Amazingly, in each of the above situations I was offering the exact same things. The only thing that changed was the time allotted to the authors I worked with to finish their books. That's it. And the plans associated with the different timeframes I offered all came to me at different times and in the same way— divine inspiration received while I was in my DAW state working with authors. Yes, looking back, I feel that these descending time periods were the result of a divine inspiration I had received. Those divine inspirations were in response to an ever-expanding consciousness to the God within us all, trying desperately to birth a message and dying to be born through the books many of us feel drawn to write.

What's the secret behind the amazing results I have not only experienced but witnessed firsthand? Reconnecting and then remaining connected to God, both as a writer and as a human being, and then allowing one's DAW to express itself through the books so many of us are compelled to write.

Chapter Two

Why Haven't You Been Able to Fully Birth Your Book to Your Potential?

OKAY, SO HERE YOU ARE AT LEAST RELATIVELY smart, honest, hardworking, and committed. You have probably graduated from schools or programs, successfully held jobs, paid taxes, possibly paid off loans, built things from homes to relationships, raised kids, et cetera. Yet, the thing you could possibly want to do for yourself more than anything else, write a book, you have been unsuccessful at completing.

Maybe you're just not talented, experienced, educated enough to do so, or maybe it is simply not in the cards for you. Bull! We may not all look, think, or live alike, but one thing that each one of us has the capability to do is write. Yes, it can be that natural for all of us and it is a God-given right not just because it supplies an essential opportunity to become one with the Creator but also because it is the one route we all share to deliver some form of divine message we were at least partially born to birth. So natural and innate is the ability to write that even someone with the physical liabilities of Stephen Hawking can do so, and do so very effectively. If it is so natural, innate, and easy to do then why have you not been able to do so to a satisfactory or publishable level?

First of all, in response, let me say this: "It has nothing to do with you and everything to do with you." What do I mean by that? Second, the motivation to take the wrong turn that steered you away from the ease that writing could be did not originate inside you. As noted in the introduction, it came directly from what you were taught about writing and publishing.

In reality, you were taught the exact opposite about what you needed to know to succeed as a writer. How could that be? The curriculums that most influenced you in this area were designed by individuals—as caring, intelligent and accredited as they were—who hadn't studied the art form of writing from a holistic perspective, and thus didn't have a full understanding of it. What do I mean by holistic perspective of writing? Doesn't holistic have to do with the New Age or organic produce or something?

By holistic, I am referring to the four arenas of writing: the physical, mental, spiritual, and emotional aspects. What we are normally taught about writing comes from the mental perspective only. So, what we have been taught and forced to absorb about writing to get that all-important passing grade is one-dimensional. What we have been taught would be like trying to drive a car with only one inflated tire. Doing so would be frustrating, dangerous, and slow. After trying to drive a car with three flat tires, most of us would just give up. This is essentially what most aspiring authors do.

However, with all four tires properly inflated, which is what this book will do for the writing of your book, the car rolls nicely, and potentially quickly, just as your book will.

Third, it's all about you because up until this point, you have innocently chosen to accept the misinformation you were offered on writing as the gospel. Whether you choose to fully embrace the proven solutions in this book will be up to you. It's all about you— always has been and always will be.

"We are dancing on a volcano."

—COMTE DE SALVANDY

Chapter Three

What Caused Our DAWs to Go into Hiding in the First Place?

Yes, the truth is that there are many outside factors that attempt to influence your free will, but realistically, you are the only one who can keep your dreams from becoming a reality.

"The potential for natural writing is already within all of us; it is not too late for any of us to learn," claims Gabriele Rico in her bestselling book, *Writing the Natural Way*.

If outside influences were really as dominant as we make them, then people such as Maya Angelou (who worked her way out of the ghetto to become one of the most respected writers in modern history), Frank McCourt (who rose from a severely dysfunctional upbringing to become a bestselling author), and others from our society who have walked similar roads, would have never ended up where they did.

Fears

> "Whether you think you can, or you think you can't, you're right."
>
> —HENRY FORD

No matter what the cost or what barriers stand between them and their dreams, some people just choose to follow their inner voice, their DAWs: that magical, all-knowing connection they hear calling them forward. Others respond to another voice, which I refer to as the Holy Ego (HE), that logical/critical calling of outside influences telling them to "stand still," "don't move," or even worse, "turn tail and run!" Why is it that anyone would allow his or her essential connection with his or her true self, the DAW, to be severed? The answer is simple. They were conditioned to do just that.

It Begins When Society Tries to Sever Your DAW Connection

Supposedly, the security and strength of a society is based upon the cohesiveness of its individual members—the abilities of its members to fall in line, to conform. Thus, even though at one time in your life—probably as a child—you wouldn't have considered not adhering to the expressions of your DAW connection, eventually societal pressures that were too large to resist were thrust upon you. It was then that your connection with your DAW, that which makes each one of us so unique and special, was broken.

No matter how powerful the calling of your DAW and no matter how strong the connection, you were outnumbered and out-positioned; you had no other choice but to give in.

"Mistakes are the portals of discovery."

—JAMES JOYCE

Parents and Others

The first attempt to get you to sever your connection came as the result of your loving parents' strict adherence to and projection of society's ways. In reality all your parents were trying to do was protect you from being an outcast. Thus, they taught you to fall in line, to be one of the pack. They also taught us what wasn't possible, what we didn't want, or at least thought we didn't want.

"Conformity is the jailer of freedom and the enemy of growth."

—JOHN F. KENNEDY

"Embarrassment, self-consciousness, remembered criticism, can stifle the average person so that less and less in his lifetime can he open himself out," says Ray Bradbury in his book *The Zen of Writing*.

"That's a nice story, Johnny. Now go do your math homework."

"It's really cute that you like to sing, Judy, but remember a nurse is what you want to be."

"Do you want to have a big house and nice car like Mommy and Daddy? If you do, you better get your grades up, because authors don't make any money."

"Oh, she'll grow out of it and come to her senses. She doesn't really want to be an actor.

She's way too smart for that."

"I'm really worried about him, Bob. He just sits there scribbling down story after story."

So many of our seeds land upon hard ground, and thus, in this all-too-common situation, are unable to survive beyond childhood. They oftentimes have to wait until adulthood, when we are finally able to sprout on our own. This awakening is often perceived as a crisis, a mid-life crisis.

"Only a few of us keep on expressing this need through a sustained relationship with language, our natural urge for self-expression inhibited by the weight of rules and prescriptions," says Rico.

"There's a black sheep in every flock."

—PROVERB

Misconceptions and BS

The misinformation flows at a greater pace as we move further and further up the educational ladder. The more formal education one acquires, the more misinformation he or she absorbs. "Our American professors like their literature clear and cold and pure and very dead," said author Sinclair Lewis.

> "Teach your children that they will never be judged, that they need not worry about always getting it right, and that they do not have to change anything, or 'get better,' to be seen as perfect and beautiful in the eyes of God."
>
> —NEALE DONALD WALSCH
>
> *Communion with God*

"People at the top of the tree are those without qualifications to detain those at the bottom," claims Peter Ustinov. The higher we climb, the more inappropriate information we are expected to absorb, all of which severs deeper and deeper our necessary DAW connection.

"Education is simply the soul of a society as it passes from one generation to another," G. K. Chesterton once wrote.

"Most books on writing are filled with bullshit," claims bestselling author Stephen King in his book *On Writing: A Memoir of the Craft*. "Fiction writers, present company included, don't even understand very much about what they do—not why it works when it's good, not why it doesn't when it's bad," continues King.

"Education made us what we are," writes Claude-Adrien Helvetius.

"Our principal writers have nearly all been fortunate in escaping regular education," says Hugh Macdiarmid.

"Creative minds always have been known to survive any kind of bad training," claimed Anna Freud.

All this criticism we are exposed to eventually leads to unnecessary worries that snowball with the further absorption of more misconceptions and, as King puts it, "bullshit," which eventually creates unnecessary fears, including fearing what we want most out of life.

Fear of Success

> "Let me assert my firm belief that the only thing we have to fear is fear itself."
>
> —FRANKLIN D. ROOSEVELT

When I first began teaching, I distributed a questionnaire to my students. To be able to address their individual and cumulative situations, I needed to know what made them tick.

More than anything else, I needed to know what had kept these successful individuals, who paid their taxes, held jobs, raised families, and who had graduated from schools, from achieving an equal amount of success with their writing.

Much to my surprise, the majority of persons whom

I surveyed feared what they wanted most. Of course, in a perfect and/or functional world this would not be the case.

If you are anything at all like the population represented in that survey—even though the alteration in your expressive lifestyle might bring you everything that you personally seek—you could have an even greater fear tied to a loss of your privacy and anonymity that stands in the way.

> "But I do nothing upon myself, and yet I am my own Executioner."
>
> —JOHN DONNE

You might worry that if you become a success, your friends, spouse, and family, with whom you fear your relationships are conditional (as opposed to unconditional), would no longer like or love you, or they would envy you and thus despise you.

> "People hate me because I am a multifaceted, talented, wealthy, internationally famous genius."
>
> JERRY LEWIS

You could also fear reprisals, which you might have experienced on previous occasions. Where would reactions that are the opposite of what we would expect come from? They are born out of a constant connection with a scared, and thus conditional society, and all those who have been exposed to it, including our family and friends, our business associates, and the educational system. Is it any wonder then that the possibility of having what we truly want has actually frightened us away from acquiring it at times?

> "Lend voices only to sounds of freedom. No longer lend your strength to that which you wish to be free from."
>
> —JEWEL

I have provided some of the typical responses I received to the survey below. Read through the list of replies and mark any that cause you to feel some sort of reaction, no matter what it might be. After you have done that, turn on the subliminal portion (track 2) of the *Transitioning Back into the Author You Were Meant to Be* CD you downloaded from my website. Make sure you have your large blank pad of paper next to you along with a pen or two.

Then take a few minutes to get into a relaxed state: sit up comfortably straight, make sure your arms and legs are uncrossed, take a few deep breaths, and exhale as deeply as you can; smile, and hold that smile for a minute or so.

Smiling and laughing sends a message to our brains that everything must be okay, that we are safe, otherwise, we wouldn't be smiling and laughing. Smile, and keep your eyes closed for a few minutes while doing so. Keeping your eyes closed directs your consciousness inward, which is exactly where we want it to go. Without the distractions of the outside world, which are now taken away—we are such a visually based culture—it has nowhere else to go.

After you have allowed yourself to sink into relaxation for a few moments, open your eyes and read over the first statement you marked. Then close your eyes, take a few deep breaths, and exhale even more deeply and allow yourself to fully feel whatever it is that comes through you in response to that statement.

Once you are fully one with your response to this statement, open your eyes and write down, no matter how long it takes, whatever you are feeling. Then perform these same steps with any of the other statements you might have marked as well.

There is no specific timeframe associated with this exercise. Date and record your feelings in your lined notebook.

"The only true happiness comes from squandering ourselves for a purpose."

—WILLIAM COOPER

Examples of Fears of Success—
The Two Directions

Fears of Change

"If I succeed, I will be expected to continue to do so, and I'm not sure that I will be able to follow through. So, wouldn't it be just a whole heck of a lot easier to avoid all of the embarrassment and hassle by not even attempting to succeed in the first place?"

"Hey, I've been living the same style of life for as long as I can remember. I've had the same job for years. I've lived in the same house and the same town for what seems like forever. My life may not be everything I want it to be, but no one can guarantee me that it wouldn't be worse were I to risk going after what it is that I think I really want."

"Successful persons are always on the go. They're always doing something, touring here or there. They have wealth and esteem. Everybody knows them, and I'm just not cut out for all that stuff."

"People will know more about me than I am comfortable with them knowing."

"I'll be seen as being crazy."

"I will look like a fool."

"The world likes the little guy. It's the guy with all the money and fame that it dislikes. Assassinations are reserved for those with power and fame. No one has ever heard of a nobody being attacked for who they were."

"The illusion of Failure is necessary in order to experience the exhilaration of Success."

—NEALE DONALD WALSCH

Communion with God

Fears of Loss

"Those closest to me just won't understand me anymore, and there's nothing that I value more than their company, attention, and affection."

"If I end up where it is that I want to go, for the first time in my life I will have something that I will love, and thus, I will fear losing it."

"My life might be far from perfect, but at least I am in control of it. If I were to succeed, there is no doubt that I would lose the structure I need to live, exist, and that is just not acceptable."

"I will be hounded by all sorts of responsibilities. I will no longer have my own time, my own life."

"I will be overtaken by my love for what it is I do, and I won't be able to continue to fulfill my obligations to those around me. As a result, they will eventually end up disliking me or possibly even leaving me."

"I would have to leave those I love to do what I want to do."

Our Deepest Fear

"Our doubts are traitors, and make us lose the good we oft might win by fearing to attempt."

—SHAKESPEARE

Take a few moments once again either to get into or to establish your relaxed state. Then open your eyes and read over the following quote written by Marianne Williamson, allowing the words to sink deeply into you.

Our deepest fear is not that we are inadequate.

Our deepest fear is that we are

Powerful beyond measure.

It is our Light, not our

Darkness that most frightens us.

We ask ourselves, Who am I to be brilliant,

Gorgeous, talented, and fabulous?

Actually, who are you not to be?

You are a child of God.

Your playing small does not serve the world.

There is nothing enlightened about

Shrinking so that other people

Will not feel insecure around you.

We were all meant to shine, as children do.

We were born to make manifest the

Glory of God that is within us.

It is not just in some of us; it is in everyone and

As we let our own light shine,

We unconsciously give others

Permission to do the same.

As we are liberated from our own fear,

Our presence automatically

Liberates others.

—MARIANNE WILLIAMSON

A Return to Love

How do you feel? Express whatever it is you are feeling on your large blank pad of paper, writing as fast as you can and allowing your Divine Author Within to be the guide. Then date and record your reaction in your lined notebook.

"To feel themselves in the presence of true greatness many men find it necessary only to be alone."

—TOM MASSON

Examples of Fears of Failure

You may find this to be strange but I have found that it is not fear of failure, but rather fear of success, to be the most prevalent or controlling in those drawn to writing. Why is this so? Maybe it's because we live in a society based on "trial and error" and have grown used to, accustomed to, this sort of experience. As a result it does not inhibit us as much as our own success. Perhaps the act of sharing our deepest and most personal and real selves just makes us so much more vulnerable to the jealousies and inappropriate trainings of others in this regard, such that our fear of success couldn't help but be stronger.

I don't know the reason why you have been so paralyzed by your fears of success.

> "When people do not respect us we are sharply offended; yet deep down in his private heart no man much respects himself."
>
> —MARK TWAIN

Quite possibly, you might be able to differentiate between which of these two major offspring of fear affect you the most, as well as why one of these major catalysts is stronger, by entering into the same exercise with the following statements that you used with the Fears of Success listed previously.

Make sure to date and record your results in your notebook. The Fears of Failure, which came out in my survey, fell primarily into one category.

> "The failure of outer things to satisfy leads the soul to seek the power within."
>
> —BAIRD T. SPALDING
>
> *Life and Teaching of the Masters*
> *Of The Far East*

> "If God created us in His own image, we have more than reciprocated."
>
> —VOLTAIRE

Fear of Failure

Fear of Lack

> "No one would be interested in what I'd have to say or do anyway."

> "Anything that I would try on my own wouldn't work."

> "No matter what I do I always wind up screwing up."

"I have a difficult time believing that I deserve anything good in my life."

"I'm not smart enough."

"I don't have enough money."

"I'm not attractive enough."

"I'm not brave enough."

"I'm not dedicated enough."

"I'm not serious enough."

"I don't have good luck."

"I haven't paid my dues."

"I'm not talented enough."

"I'm too old."

"I'm too young."

"I don't have anything to say."

"Who would want to hear what I have
to say anyway?"

"Obstacles are those frightful things you see
when you take your eyes off your goal."

—HENRY FORD

The Man or Woman in the Mirror:

"The heart has its reasons, which reason knows
not."

—BLAISE PASCAL

The Good News Is You Can Reverse It

It is up to you to decide what it is that you will
do with your writing and what you will allow your
writing to do with your life. If you so choose, now is
the time to take back control and move swiftly and
joyfully in the direction of your dreams and aspirations,
no matter what they are.

Just as a light socket responds only to a certain
fitting of bulb, you won't be able to make the proper

connection unless you begin seeing yourself as your DAW, and thus God, or however you refer to him/her/it, sees you in all your brilliance, love, and wonder. That's step one, a step of self-reconnection.

The following exercise, which works like a salve in removing these core infections, is designed to help you do just that. To do the exercise, you will need a mirror, your large drawing pad, pens, and some sort of system that will allow you to play the *Transitioning* CD as you go through the exercise.

You are encouraged to stay with this exercise for however many sessions are necessary until you can look yourself in the eye, repeat the following statements, and literally feel nothing at all.

> "There is a road from the eye to the heart that does not go through the intellect."
>
> —G. K. CHESTERTON

Then and only then will the effects of the previous fears have been cleansed from your psyche. Then and only then will you be prepared to move forward.

Step 1: Position yourself in front of a mirror.

> "A novel is a mirror carried along a high road."
>
> —STENDHAL

Step 2: Take time to close your eyes, clear your mind, and relax.

> "The only service a friend can really render is to keep up your courage by holding up to you a mirror in which you can see a noble image of yourself."
>
> —GEORGE BERNARD SHAW

Step 3: Open your eyes and using the mirror look yourself directly in the eyes. Repeat the first statement allowing any and all thoughts or feelings to spill out onto your paper. After you have done that, repeat the statement again. Allow whatever arises to spill onto the paper again. Do this over and over and over again until, as mentioned, you can look yourself in the eye, repeat the statement, and feel nothing. Then move to the next statement and do the same thing. Once you have completed your work with statement number two, follow the same steps with the third statement, fourth, and then the fifth and final one. Do not move on to the next chapter until you can look at yourself in the eyes and repeat any of the five statements and feel absolutely nothing.

Five Statements

1. *"Life is my best teacher; it provides me with all that I need to know."*

2. *"My mind is an endless storehouse of ideas and inspirations."*

3. *"I do best what I like to do most."*

4. *"What I like to do most brings me the personal success that I desire."*

5. *"What I like to do most affords me all the opportunities I desire to live my life as I choose."*

"Until you look in the mirror and see your own beliefs reflected there, you will be using every brother or sister in your experience as a mirror to show you what you believe about yourself."

—PAUL FERRINI

Love without Conditions

"I am the Roman Emperor, and am above grammar."

—SIGISMUND

Chapter Four

Ruby versus Larry

THERE ARE TWO STEPS TO REVERSING AND REPLACING an ineffective habit. First, find the reason for the habit, which is usually rooted in reaction to one of the two major forms of fear written about earlier, and needs to be uprooted. That is what the exercise in the last chapter was all about. Second, the habits associated with those former behavior patterns need to be adjusted, reversed in most cases, so your habits and behaviors will better reflect what you seek to accomplish as your divine purpose or part of that purpose.

Differentiating between those two forms of habitual actions is essential to your recovery from your past. Simply ripping a fear-based habitual sequence up by its roots is not enough. The behavior patterns that formed as a result need to be acknowledged and reversed. That

[41]

is what this chapter is all about.

Enter Nobel Prize Winner Roger W. Sperry. Roger W. Sperry and his students at the California Institute of Technology in the 1950s and 1960s devised the split-brain or right/left brain theory, for which he eventually won a Nobel Prize in Medicine in the mid 1980s. At the essence of Sperry's work is the fact that humans actually have two independently functioning brains as opposed to two lobes springing from one brain. Sperry's proof of his theory revolutionized the way people viewed how they thought, expressed themselves, and lived life.

Shortly after the release of Sperry's work, bestselling books began appearing on the shelves, such as Betty Edward's *Drawing on the Right Side of the Brain* and Gabriele Rico's *Writing the Natural Way*, which confirmed that we no longer had to suffer deprivation and frustration to pursue the arts of drawing and writing. All we had to do was know how to self-induce a DAW-based state and keep from rejecting that state after it arrived.

Even though what I am about to share has its roots in Sperry's original right/left brain theory, it has reached its own full potential for our work with the DAW as the result of my own research. Thus, I have taken the liberty of replacing some of his original terminology with my own titles.

The name Ruby is what I have chosen to call your creative, heartfelt side, through which your DAW can be accessed.

"A revolution is a struggle to the death between the future and the past."

—FIDEL CASTRO

Conversely, Larry is your logical, always-stop-at-a-stop-sign, pay-your-taxes-on-time side. Let me clarify before beginning that, no matter what your gender, you have both a Ruby and a Larry. Both also have the ability to add tremendous value to your life.

Larry

Larry, a no-nonsense type of dude, has already led you to great success in your life, and his efforts surely need to be applauded. He has led you to graduate from school, to the acquisition of degrees, to landing jobs and keeping them, to paying your bills, and stopping at stop signs—just to mention a few of the tens of thousands of achievements to which he has personally and directly led you. It would be fair to say that every success you have experienced, no matter how large or small, has come as a direct result of your Larry.

However, as much of an asset as Larry has been in so many other arenas, in the area of open, heart-felt expression and writing in particular, he has actually directly led you away from living up to your fullest potential. The reason for Larry's shortcomings in that area comes simply as the result of the fact that he both listened to and believed in what you were taught about writing.

In some cases Larry has been so effective in doing what he did for so long that he has accidently, even without his own self knowing that he was doing so, literally shut down your connection with your DAW. All of this happened as the result of your faithful friend Larry being improperly trained.

To reverse this trend in your life, and to thus achieve the results you seek with your DAW, Larry must be retrained to see your connection with your DAW and your potential work as a writer from a much different perspective. To do that, we must first better understand the makeup and true purpose and history behind Larry.

Larry's Sole Purpose: To Avoid Pain

> "It is hard to fight an enemy who has outposts in your head."
>
> —SALLY KEMPTON

When you were born, your Larry lay in a state of dormancy. Like a blank hard drive, nothing had been written upon him. All he would learn about life and his unique place in your life would come as a result of his rote and repetitious learning style, which was tied directly to his connection with your five senses. He was dependent upon them not only for stimuli but for information, the facts and figures he so liked.

During the first two years of your life, Larry learned

all about sensations and feelings. He craved peace and happiness and learned to seek out whatever situations, people, activities, or stimuli that offered what he liked best. Larry also learned to avoid that which caused any sort of pain. So painful and consistent were the rules and regulations placed upon you during your childhood that your Larry, in an attempt to protect you, took on the role of society in protecting you from anything that could in any way cause you pain.

Unfortunately, because of its uniqueness and the fact that it tended to color way outside the narrow lines that society deemed as being safe, Larry, who was just trying to do his job well, rejected your DAW and any activity of inspiration associated with it.

"The conscious mind must seek and want the spirit in order to learn the power of the spirit."

—BAIRD T. SPALDING

Life and Teaching of the Masters
Of the Far East

To keep you safe, at least from his perspective, Larry took over the directing of your life, as opposed to Ruby. From that time until the present, to both maintain his control over your life and thus to be able to keep you safe, Larry has done whatever he felt was necessary to keep you away from any form of connection at all with your DAW.

"The predominance of mind is no more than a stage in the evolution of consciousness. We need to go on to the next stage now, as a matter of urgency; otherwise, we will be destroyed by the mind, which has grown into a monster."

—ECKHART TOLLE

The Power of Now

If somehow your DAW did break through into a conscious awareness in your life, Larry would do whatever he had to do—all in the sake of keeping you safe—to interrupt that connection at all costs. If by some miracle, your DAW broke through long enough to produce a tangible result in your life (like a book), Larry was left with no other alternative than to discredit whatever it was that was produced.

"Supremacy over every discord can come only in the degree that we understand that they do not come from God."

—BAIRD T. SPALDING

Life and Teaching of the Masters Of the Far East

To best support his primary purpose, Larry is:

- **Politely Analytical, Critical, and Judgmental**—Better to be safe than sorry.

"Not to be able to stop thinking is a dreadful affliction, but we don't realize this because almost everyone is suffering from it, so it is considered normal."

—ECKHART TOLLE

The Power of Now

- **Conditional**—He is willing to participate in doing anything as long as you can guarantee results, but staunchly chooses not to participate in anything without any guaranteed, qualitative results.

- **Falsely Dominant**—Since we are taught at an early age that the key to living a successful life lies in one's ability to avoid one's fears, is it any wonder that Larry was chosen to lead as opposed to Ruby?

"Let us be thankful for the fools. But for them the rest of us could not succeed."

—MARK TWAIN

- **Forgetful**—He has a short-term memory, which is why he has chosen to learn through rote memory and repetition. He has to be exposed to something over and over again before he finally feels safe with it and learns it through a unique process of conditioning. Due to his short-term memory, Larry equates familiarity, no matter how disastrous the situation, with safety. His short-term memory is the result of a small memory capacity that oftentimes causes him to easily be overwhelmed and thus shut down by the flood of inspiration Ruby can share.

- **Limited in His Capabilities**—What would you expect of a guy with a short-term memory (STM) who relies only on what he has gathered from your five senses to see the world?

- **Tired**—With all of the stress and tension Larry is obvious under, he needs to sleep.

Ruby

As you will see, Ruby and Larry are nearly complete opposites. Ruby literally embodies the old saying:

> "Work like you don't need the money,
> love like you've never been hurt,
> and dance like no one is looking."

When the two work together, which is rare in our society, they blend together into one overwhelming performance like Fred Astaire and Ginger Rogers on the dance floor. But to get that to transpire in your life on a permanent basis, you need to do some work. Once you do the work, your life will flow like a melody.

Ruby:

- **Feels** as opposed to thinks—she's all heart, flow, rhythm, expression. That is just her.

- **Is Unconditional**—She has no concern about the outcome; she only focuses on the expression.

- **Innately Dominant**—We were all born with Ruby as our leader until she got pushed aside by unnatural fears that were forced into our life. Larry has became the leader of our lives.

"In no other period of history were the learned so mistrustful of the divine possibilities in man as they are now."

—GOPI KRISHNA

* **Has the Memory of an Elephant**—Everything she has ever experienced is permanently and safely stored away in her unlimited memory banks.

* **Possesses Unlimited Capabilities**—She can do anything and she knows it, for she comes from outside your life, from outside your body, and isn't in any way inhibited by any dependence upon your five senses.

* **Never Sleeps**—Why would she? She's here to be

alive and awake, not asleep.

> "The only man who is really free is the one who can turn down an invitation to dinner without giving an excuse."
>
> —JULES RENARD

> "Humankind cannot bear very much reality."
>
> —T. S. ELIOT

CHAPTER FIVE

HOW YOUR DAW SPEAKS TO YOU AND THROUGH YOU

OUTSIDE OF RECOGNIZING THAT INDEED YOUR DAW does exist, that you can connect with it at-will, and that it speaks through your by coming through Ruby, the next significant revelation I am about to introduce deals with the finite details of how it communicates with you through your writing. This will provide you with the confidence and power to merge into a direct interchange with it.

Archetypes

The term *archetype* was first made popular in the modern world by psychotherapist Carl Jung. Jung used the term to describe images shared with us by what he referred to as our subconscious. Due to their vivid richness and color, these images could be interpreted from many different angles, and as a result, oftentimes possessed a myriad of meanings.

To begin with, for our use, it's best to define the type of archetypes we will be working with as *symbolic representations of universal messages or meanings*.

I want to clarify right here and now that archetypes associated with your writing can surface in many different ways. For example, if you are writing fiction, these symbolic representations of universal messages and meanings may present themselves as characters.

> "I am large, I contain multitudes."
>
> —WALT WHITMAN

In non-fiction they may appear as images of yourself in former times when you were seeking the answers you now feel drawn to address, or of students or people with whom you have dealt in your life.

In fiction or non-fiction, Archetypical tones or voices may begin to surface in you that perhaps never showed before and now seem to surface only when writing or when writing on a specific subject. As important as it is that you understand the use of archetypes in your writing by your DAW—so you consciously go with the DAW flow as opposed to hesitate getting involved—I will not spend a laborious amount of time on this subject. The reason being that Larry can become addicted, and in doing so use his reaction to this material to actually keep you from giving into your DAW. He will get lost, kind of like what he does with a Rubik's Cube. That, of course, is not the purpose of this or any chapter in this book.

I will go over a basic understanding of what it is that you need to know, just so you don't get surprised by what transpires in your interactions with your DAW, which would stop you from going any farther.

The third major point I want to make is that there are two archetypes: transitional archetypes and primary archetypes.

> "When I want to read a novel, I write one."
>
> —BENJAMIN DISRAELI

Transitional Archetypes

Transitional archetypes, or TAs as I call them, exist for the simple purpose of educating you through the removal of biases that Larry has which have been holding you back. TAs almost always appear as a feeling or as a result of an image of someone you know, love, or trust.

Don't flip out if you begin writing a racy romance and an image of your grandmother shows up. Your grandmother is not going to be in your book, or at least I hope not. Her image, as projected by your DAW, is only showing up to teach Larry something (because you both eventually have to work together here to succeed) that will educate him, so that a bias can then be removed and you can both surge forward together.

You may experience the presentation of only one TA before actually beginning a book (remember, don't confuse the appearance of a TA with writing a book). Perhaps there may be several or maybe none at all. Perhaps Larry doesn't need to drop any formerly helpful bias before you both surge forward.

TAs almost always make their appearances before the presentation of any primary archetypes, or PAs. It is simply the TA's job to clear the path for the PAs, whose voice, mannerisms, and style, even if they just appear as a certain projection, will actually become the authors of your books.

Primary Archetypes

If they appear so directly, PAs actually surface in the visual form of a person or character, or can also appear in the form of a voice, swagger, or tone that seems to come through you. If a group of people you have never seen before appear in your mind and have seemingly taken over your fingers, and they get you to start writing what it is that they want to say, and you end up writing a novel, that is a normal PA experience.

If past images of a student, co-worker, someone you once knew, or an earlier image of yourself appears and you begin writing (let's say a how-to book) to address his or her or their needs, that would be reflective of a primary archetypical experience as well.

According to Keats, the description of Apollo in the

third book of his epic poem *Hyperion* came to him "by chance or magic—to be, as it were, something given to me." Keats added that he had "not been aware of the beauty of some thought or expression until after I had composed and written it down." It then struck him with "astonishment" and seemed "rather the production of another person" than himself.

"In most men there exists a poet who died young, whom the man survived," said Sainte-Beuve.

"Know that there is often hidden in us a dormant poet, always young and alive," seconded de Must.

"Let us now consider the Personal Daemon," began Rudyard Kipling.

> Most men, and some most unlikely, keep him under an alias which varies with their literary or scientific attainments. Mine came to me early when I sat bewildered among other notions, and said; 'Take this and no other.' I obeyed, and was rewarded. . .
>
> After that I learned to lean upon him and recognize the sign of his approach. If ever I held back, Ananias fashion, anything of myself (even though I had to throw it out afterwards) I paid for it by missing what I then knew the tale lacked. . .
>
> My Daemon was with me in *The Jungle Books*, *Kim*, and both *Puck* books, and good care I took to walk delicately, lest he should withdraw. I know that he did not, because when those books were finished they said so themselves with, almost, the water-hammer click of a tap turned off. Note here. When your Daemon is in charge, do not try

to think consciously. Drift, wait, and obey.

In his memoirs, Robert Louis Stevenson quite candidly personified this state as an experienced cadre of dream helpers he called his "Brownies," and explained how he came to use and finally to exploit them. Stevenson had a bit to say about them in a little-known essay entitled "A Chapter on Dreams."

"Through surrender, spiritual energy comes into the world."

—ECKHART TOLLE

The Power of Now

The more I think of it, the more I am moved to press upon the world my question: Who are the Little People? They are near connections of the dreamer's, beyond doubt; they share in his financial worries and have an eye to the bank-book; they share plainly in his training; they have plainly learned like him to build the scheme of a considerate story and to arrange emotion in progressive order; only I think they have more talent; and one thing is beyond doubt, they can tell him a story piece by piece, like a serial, and keep him all the while in ignorance of where they aim. Who are they, then? And who is the dreamer?

Well, as regards the dreamer, I can answer that, for he is no less a person than myself . . . and for the Little People, what shall I say they are but just my Brownies, God bless them! who do one-half my work for me while I am fast asleep, and in all human likelihood, do the rest for me as well, when I am wide awake and fondly suppose I do it for myself. That part which is done while I am sleeping is the Brownies' part beyond contention; but that which is done when I am up and about is by no means necessarily mine, since all goes to show the Brownies have a hand in it even then. I am an excellent advisor, something like Moliere's servant; I pull back and I cut down; and I dress the whole in the best words and sentences that I can find and make; I hold the pen, too; and I do the sitting at the table, which is about the worst of it; and when all is done, I make up the manuscript and pay for the registration; so that, on the whole, I have some claim to share, though not so largely as I do, in the profits of our common enterprise.

"Literature is mostly about having sex and not much about having children; life is the other way round."

—DAVID LODGE

I can but give an instance or so of what part is done sleeping and what part awake, and leave the reader to share what laurels there are, at his own nod, between myself and my collaborators; and to do this I will first take a book that a number of persons have been polite enough to read, *The Strange Case of Dr. Jekyll and Mr. Hyde*. I had long been trying to write a story on this subject, to find a body, a vehicle, for that strong sense of man's double being which must at times come in upon and overwhelm the mind of every thinking creature. I had even written one, *The Travelling Companion*, which was returned by an editor on the pleas that it was a work of genius and indecent, and which I burned the other day on the ground that it was not a work of genius, and that *Jekyll* had supplanted it. Then came one of those financial fluctuations to which (with an elegant modesty) I have hitherto referred in the third person. For two days I went about racking my brains for a plot of any sort; and on the second night I dreamed the scene at the window, and a scene afterward split in two, in which Hyde, pursued for some crime, took the powder and underwent the change in the presence of his pursuers. All the rest was made awake, and consciously, although I think I can trace in much of it the manner of my Brownies.

"There is surely a piece of divinity in us, something that was before the elements."

—THOMAS BROWNE

Enough said. It is important to both understand and grasp this concept. You don't want to impede on your own progress as an author by rejecting this routine form of communication from your DAW. Again, to further belabor the points made already in this chapter would just open the door for Larry to get lost in trying to understand it. The most important understandings to walk away from this chapter with are:

- Your DAW will attempt to communicate with you and your readers through the types of images you have routinely experienced in dreams; these are referred to as archetypes.

- There are two forms of archetypes—transitional archetypes (TAs) and primary archetypes (PAs).

- TAs exist for the sole purpose of removing Larry's biases and making room for your PAs and your book to come through.

- The appearance of an archetypical association in your writing is normal; in fact, it is so normal that if one did not appear, there would be room for concern that you were not directly plugging into your DAW.

CHAPTER SIX

THE POWER OF BREAKTHROUGHS

"Lord, deliver me from myself!"

—THOMAS BROWNE

THE LIFE-TRANSFORMING DIFFERENCE THAT CAN transpire as the result of connecting with your Divine Author Within is all around us. Persons, such as bestselling author John Grisham, were able to break through all of the dogma and succeed not only financially but retain personal virtues as a result of consciously giving in to this connection. Grisham was a struggling attorney with no formal training in writing before opening up to his DAW and listening to It through his Ruby. All of this paid off in a worldwide influence for him—his books, of course, have made hundreds of millions of dollars worth of sales.

What was Stephen King doing during the time when he totally gave into his DAW connection? Menial jobs, anything that would earn him the income he needed to survive, but nothing more. Then his book sales took off. Oh, did they take off.

Andrew Greeley was a priest. Tom Clancy was in business.

> "Strange fits of passion have I known."
>
> —WILLIAM WORDSWORTH

Anthony Robbins was too young and didn't even have a real job yet. In the world of music, Mozart felt the DAW and welcomed it, which allowed him to brilliantly express himself through his music at an age when all other would-be composers were still playing with blocks. Beethoven felt it, recognized it, and gave in to it, which is why he was able to compose his most masterful symphony, even after he had gone totally deaf. In the business arena, modern icons such as media magnate Ted Turner, the czar of the ever-expanding computer industry, Bill Gates, and many others, rode their callings to success and set their respective fields afire, changing life as we know it.

In his book *My Life and the Beautiful Game*, the great soccer player Pele described the state in this fashion: "I felt a strange calmnes. . . a kind of euphoria. I felt I could run all day without tiring, that I could dribble through any of their team or all of them, that I could almost pass through them physically. I felt I could not be hurt. It was a strange feeling and one I had not felt before. Perhaps it was merely confidence, but I have felt confident many times without that strange feeling of invincibility."

> "Remove the illusions, lift the veil, and you will rest in the heart. Rest in the heart, and God will abide with you."
>
> —PAUL FERRINI
>
> *Return to the Garden*

Again, in the world of writing, this connection is especially prevalent and available. While at one with his connection, Jack Kerouac wrote his finest works in only a few sleepless days.

> "In heaven an angel is nobody in particular."
>
> —GEORGE BERNARD SHAW

Ernest Hemingway felt so excited and stimulated that he wrote while standing up. Thomas Wolfe did the same, and since he was so tall, actually did his writing on the top of an icebox. Samuel Beckett, the award-winning playwright, wrote his cornerstone of modern drama, *Waiting for Godot*, in a mere few months while in this state. Singer/songwriter Harry Chapin wrote his 1970s blockbuster hit "Taxi" in less than thirty minutes while standing in a subway.

You have been there yourself—have you not?—

when the pen has literally jumped out of your hand, covering what felt like miles of once impassable, blank space in bliss-laden seconds. So you have already experienced this. You realize the intimidating power of a connection such as the ones illustrated above. You also know then that you are capable of having it.

An aspiring author of mine, while in this state and working on the completion of her first book, wrote over 25,000 words, the equivalent of 85 double-spaced pages, in one day. Another completed over 17,000 in the same period of time. In both cases, their works, upon being edited, were found to be nearly without flaw.

I spoke to the former of the two students immediately after she had completed her day of work.

"You must be tired," I probed.

"Well," she replied, with pretty much the same spark in her voice in which she had started the day, "I could go out dancing. I'm not too tired to go out to dinner or to attend a movie. Frankly, I am not physically, mentally, or emotionally tired at all. I'm just tired of writing."

I have seen hundreds complete their entire books in only a few days. Hundreds of aspiring authors attend my retreats every year and complete the writing of their books in a weekend. That's how quickly your entire life and career can change.

Yeah, but who are you to be worthy enough to have such a life-altering experience/revelation? The true question to again ask yourself is who are you not to have such a life-altering experience?

Now all you have to learn is how to allow yourself to stay with this connection long enough to give it time to elevate your life in all areas for the better.

So, what is it like to stay in this connected state for an extended period of time?

"First of all, it's a daydream, a kind of rumination about a person, a situation, something that occurs only in the mind," says author Mario Vargas Llasa. "Up until now, it's been pretty much the same with all of my books. I never get the feeling that I've decided rationally, cold blooded to write a story. On the contrary, certain events or people, sometimes dreams or readings

impose themselves suddenly and demand attention."

"When the language lends itself to me, when it comes and submits, when it surrenders and says—'I am yours, darling'—that's the best part," claims bestselling author Maya Angelou.

"Biting my taunt pen, beating myself for spite, 'Fool,' said my Muse to me, 'look in thy heart and write,'" Sir Philip Sidney wrote.

"He writes as fast as they can read, and does not write himself down," author William Hazlitt said of the experience.

"Then rising with Aurora's light, the Muse invoked, 'sit down to write,'" adds Jonathan Swift.

Who or what is it that is coming through you while in this state? You already have my answer to that question. Here are some other viewpoints as well.

"Now this creative power I think is the Holy Ghost," clarifies Brenda Ueland, author of *If You Want to Write*.

> My theology may not be very accurate but that is how I think of it. I know that William Blake called this creative power the Imagination and he said it was God. He, if anyone, ought to know, for he was one of the greatest poets and artists that ever lived.

> Blake thought this creative power should be kept alive in all people for all of their lives. And so do I. Why? Because it is life itself. It is the Spirit. In fact it is the only important thing about us. The rest of us is legs and stomach, materialistic cravings and fears.

"God has written all the books," claimed esteemed author Samuel Butler.

"Language is one of those God-given gifts that we often take for granted," says Hal Zina Bennett in his book *Write from the Heart*.

Chapter Seven

How to Get in a DAW State and Stay There Long Enough for a Book to be Born

DESPITE HOW DIFFICULT IT MAY HAVE BEEN SO FAR IN your life to not only induce, but most of all sustain a DAW state, it really doesn't have to be that challenging. In fact, it can be quite easy and take as short as just a few minutes. You heard me right. The writer's block you may have been suffering from for decades can be cured in as little as a few minutes.

How you ask? Very simple. Play both tracks A and B consecutively from the *Transitioning* CD. As mentioned, this CD has already led tens of thousands to the successful completion of their books and thus the transitions in their lives that we have already been spoken about.

The effectiveness of the CD is that it directly

counterbalances the negative effects of that which we have been taught, learned, or told about writing. It does so by following the principles of what I refer to as The Three Rs of Writing, which equate to:

1. **Reserving** a time just for your writing;

2. **Removing** any and all distractions from the environment in which you will do your writing; and

3. **Relaxing.** The idea of relaxing is very important. When you relax Larry nods off to sleep. Remember, Ruby never sleeps. Then there is no longer anything or anyone trying to stop you from making your DAW connection.

Once in your DAW state, the second side of the CD, B, will keep you there, enabling your book to continually flow out of you and offer you the consistency you need to make the personal/spiritual transition a reality. It is with that side of the CD playing that your book(s) will be written.

Getting into the DAW state and staying there directly addresses about 95 percent of the problems you could run into in the authoring of your book. The other 5 percent of the problems are covered, offering you a 100 percent solution. This is why the method works so well in helping you to write a book and in transitioning back into your real self. The other essential 5 percent of the solution is covered by the following suggestions. It is absolutely essential to employ the remaining 5 percent. Not doing so would be like not addressing an infection. Even though you may feel really good while being in 95 percent health, it is when that 5 percent, the infection, starts to take over that you start losing ground on the healthy side. The next thing you know you will be only 30 to 40 percent healthy—really sick.

Here is what makes up the essential 5 percent of the 100 percent solution: large lineless sheets of paper. By nature, your Divine Author Within is unconditional. Thus, it doesn't do well with non-universally created rules and regulations, even like lines and margins on pieces of paper and initially, at least in the beginning, the tiny spaces made available on computer monitors referred to as pages.

The DAW loves freedom to express, the wide-open spaces, which is why you were asked to purchase the large drawing pad. You will begin writing your book on this pad, until your DAW is fully birthed and you are comfortable with it. Then you can transfer your efforts to the keyboard.

The DAW's lust for the wide-open spaces can be illustrated by the fact that children, who have yet to be drawn over to Ruby's side, love to write on walls (handing them a piece of large, lineless paper, can prevent this mess from happening). William Faulkner's obsession with writing on walls, and the fact that Walt Disney created his empire by first sketching everything out, from Mickey Mouse to

Disneyland, illustrates this concept.

"The intellect is always fooled by the heart."

—DUC DE LA ROCHEFOUCAULD

In fact, so important is this consideration that you should immediately return to writing on these large lineless sheets of paper any time it appears as if you have run into a slow period or stoppage in your writing. Follow side A of the aforementioned CD and then continue on to track B—which should always be on when you are writing. Go back to the large lineless sheets of paper. The combination of these things promises a DAW connection and will immediately cure any type of mental, emotional, or literary energy blockage you could run in to.

Write in longhand. This is the only way, of course, that you are going to be able to use the large lineless pieces of paper.

To effectively follow through on this you will need to use pens that get a lot of ink to their ballpoints, those that provide the greatest amount of lubrication for a smooth and fast glide. The reason for which this come into play in the next part of the solution to this 5 percent problem.

Write as fast as you can. The reason for this is simple: the faster you write the less time you have to think—right? Larry just can't write that fast.

How fast do you have to write? The question shouldn't really be how fast do you have to write as much as how fast do you write when connected to your DAW? The answer is an average of 1,500 words per hour.

If you fall below an average of 1,200 words per hour, Larry can stay up with you for at least a while. Since my experience has taught me that over 98 percent of the mistakes you could make in writing your book are directly tied to inappropriate Larry intervention, you definitely want to keep writing as fast as you can.

Besides first getting into your DAW state, the best way to maintain that state at the pace I am referring to is simply to calculate the number of words you write every fifteen minutes. If you set a goal of writing 400 words every fifteen minutes, and keep track of your results, Larry will do whatever he has to do to keep you in that state. Thus, when you remain at that pace, you will be remaining in the DAW state needed to not only complete your book but to make the transition we have been speaking about all along.

So essential is that accountability that writing outputs are checked every fifteen minutes throughout the entire Write Your Book in a Weekend retreat.

Just keep writing no matter what. Larry is going to try and creep in and inhibit the flow that your DAW embodies. He will toss as many fears and confusing suggestions your way as possible. Just keep writing.

You will at times be at a loss to recover a name, date, or figure or to supply some bit of necessary information, just leave a space for whatever it is that you need to research later and just keep writing.

No matter what, just keep writing. If at any time you stop writing, you also stop the flow and your DAW in its tracks. Then and only then can Larry, who is dancing as fast as he can, catch up. If Larry catches up he knows just what fears to hit you with to once again drop you to your emotional, mental, spiritual, and literary knees.

Don't worry. This will not always be the case. Larry, as restrictive as he has been, really does have your best interests in mind. He has just been inappropriately trained for what you are doing. But as soon as he sees the positive results you are experiencing with your book, how happy writing makes you, and how happy the results of it make not only you but others as well, he will back way off and transform into your biggest cheerleader. After all, you do need him to succeed in this life.

Always, always positively reinforce your writing efforts. Right now your protector, Larry, believes that writing a book and all that comes with it is bad and painful for you. Of course, all he knows is what he has been taught through your five senses.

It's time for an attitude adjustment. You need Larry on your side because he is the guy that makes things a reality in this world. So how do you do that? Simple. Create a simple series of positive reinforcements attached to your writing so he can begin identifying writing as a positive thing. It's called creative reparenting.

Here's what you do. Every time you complete any

sort of writing output, no matter now grandiose or small, reward yourself with some sort of positive reinforcement—something sweet, a glass of wine, whatever—and always, always some reassuring. Here is an example: "Good job, Tom, on your writing. For doing such a good job you get..."

Larry will catch on instantly. Almost overnight writing will become a good thing in his mind and he will begin leading you to it as opposed to away from it. What a major change that will be! When that happens, all of the energy you would normally put into fighting him off will then be transferred to your writing efforts and you will really take off. For this reason it is essential to always positively reinforce your writing efforts.

Don't read, edit, or judge what you are writing, especially while you are writing. When reading is done, especially at the speed most of us are writing, we immediately slow down our consciousness to a speed at which Larry can keep up. Then the cruel, unusual, critical, and oftentimes damaging judgment occurs. As a result, what you are writing will be reduced to a pile of raw, bloody, painfully bruised flesh. If you have already done some writing, you have probably already experienced this in one form or another.

This, of course, wouldn't necessarily hold true if you were to speed-read your text. However, why even allow Larry any exposure to anything that you are writing, which he would just love to rip apart word by word?

"All of Jesus' healings were on the basis of removing the mental cause."

—BAIRD T. SPALDING

*Life and Teaching of the Masters
Of the Far East*

So important is this rule that I strongly advise my authors not to do any outside reading of any sort, even in their spare time, while writing a book. Why? Larry will use the opportunity to gain further fuel for his already out-of-control fire by adversely comparing what you have written against something written by someone else. As a result, he will try to force your DAW to write in the fashion of someone else. Who needs that? Reading someone else's material while writing your own also eats up memory and space in your consciousness that could be better used by your DAW.

Always write what you feel, no matter how displaced and unusual Larry may believe it to be at times. This is essential to getting into and remaining in a DAW-connected state. It is only when we write what we "think" that we welcome Larry back into the process and things get really confusing, dysfunctional, and painful.

Make a commitment to succeed. One of the greatest reasons that those who attend my retreats are so successful is because they make a commitment to succeed by placing on the table their time, energy, and finances. They usually also go public, at least in their own little circles, about going to the retreat and what they plan to accomplish there, which is essential.

Other than attending one of my retreats, how do you solidify the necessary commitment you need to succeed with writing your book and all that goes with it? Simple. You enter into a commitment with yourself to write it and then send that commitment to three people who you can count on to remind you about failing if you don't follow through (this, of course, can be very motivating to move beyond whatever fears you may have). Then send it to two people who love you unconditionally—you know, your best cheerleaders.

The cheerleaders just won't be as effective as the other three to whom you send a copy of your written commitment. The reason is simply that the cheerleaders will love you no matter what. The truth is you need to counteract the fears that could hold you back from not finishing the process and your book with an even greater fear: having to face one of the initial three as a failure. In that regard, the presence of these three people in your life will accomplish miracles for you.

If you would like a greater understanding of some of the secondary characteristics of what I have mentioned above and how each can be specifically handled, I would suggest visiting my website. Under the "Free" tab you can download a copy of my "Seventeen Principles of Writing." Living within the safe confines of these principles will keep both your book and personal transition flowing. If you run into a problem with your writing at any time, you can just go back to these seventeen principles, scan over them, find which one you are in innocent violation of, make the necessary adjustments to be in line with it, and you will be back on the road again to a smooth and successful completion of your book and the transition associated with it.

CHAPTER EIGHT

MEETING YOUR AUTHOR WITHIN

"If at first the idea is not absurd, then there is no hope for it."

—ALBERT EINSTEIN

IT'S TIME. YOU'VE READ ENOUGH, HEARD ENOUGH, maybe even studied and/or pondered a bit. It's time to go where you've already been. Perhaps you didn't recognize the place for what it really was, but it's time to return home to the place in our souls from which we all originated. It's time to reconnect with our truest selves, who we really are, no matter how strange that may feel at this time in your life.

From this place will come the wisdom and love, the message you were born to share with every word, action, heartbeat, and breath you take. From this place will come the personal and universal healing necessary to make your dreams a reality.

By now you should have downloaded the *Transitioning Back to the Author You Were Meant to Be* CD from my website. If you haven't already done so, go there and do it now. Make sure your large drawing pad is handy, along with some smooth-flowing pens. Make sure you are in a place where you will be undisturbed for twenty minutes or longer. In this quiet place make sure there is a straight-backed chair and a device to play the *Transitioning* CD. Then turn on the first track of the CD and follow the instructions. Allow the CD to roll on into the second track. Once the CD rolls into the subliminal second track, follow the instructions below.

You can repeat this exercise as many times as you choose before moving on to the next chapter, until you get very comfortable with your DAW.

Meeting Your Author Within

> "My dear, I don't care what they do, so long as they don't do it in the street and frighten the horses."
>
> —MRS. PATRICK CAMPBELL

Step 1: Sit up straight in your chair with your eyes closed, your head dropped to your chest, and your arms and your legs uncrossed.

> "I know I am God because when I pray to him I find I'm talking to myself."
>
> —PETER BARNES

Step 2: Allow an image of great depth to appear in your consciousness depicting when you first recognized, for whatever reason, you were being drawn to write. One at a time, ask yourself the following questions:

1. How old were you at the time?

2. Where were you?

3. What was it that you were wearing?

4. Was anyone else there?

5. What time of year was it?

6. What time of day?

7. What was it—an incident, a person, whatever—that had caused you to want to be so creative?

8. What was it that you were doing?

9. What was it that you remember most about this incident?

10. What was it that compelled you to want to write?

11. Why is it, in general, that you want to write?

Step 3: Open your eyes, pick up your pen, and allow whatever it is that you feel and remember to be released onto the sheet of lineless paper before you.

> "Surrender is inner acceptance of what is without any reservations."
>
> —ECKHART TOLLE
>
> *The Power of Now*

There is no time or speed limit associated with this exercise. Just write for as long as you would like and come back or repeat this exercise as often as you would like.

Chapter Nine

Is There Really a Book inside You?

"Whenever I look inside myself, I am afraid."

—CYRIL JOAD

I WANT YOU TO ANSWER THE FOLLOWING QUESTIONS, with a yes or no answer, as directly and quickly as you can.

1. Have you ever been writing and words poured out of you so fast that you had a difficult time keeping up?

2. Have written words ever carried with them a degree of intelligence or insight that you had a difficult time accepting as your own?

3. While taking a long drive in a car, have ideas ever flooded your mind?

4. Have you ever awakened in the middle of the night with a desire to write?

5. When you have gone away on a relaxing vacation have you ever gotten a strange urge to write?

6. Have you ever daydreamed so deeply of writing a book or screenplay that you could actually feel yourself doing it?

7. Has a story, an idea, or an urge, dying to be released, ever stuck with you for a long time and refused to let you go?

If you answered in the affirmative to any of the above, you have a book stuck inside you trying to get out. Let's find out what it is. I want you to know that during the next exercise I will be asking you to address a variety of situations. Others may come up for you as well. Please do not shy away from addressing them on your own. For this exercise, and the last one as well, you will see that you can ask whatever questions of your DAW, whether they be literary, personal, or some other segment of your life, and your Divine Author Within will respond from its uniquely spiritual and universal perspective.

The Book Inside of You

"The true God, the mighty God, is the God of ideas."

—ALFRED DE VIGNY

1. Follow the same preparatory steps taken in the previous exercise. Make sure all of your necessary tools are beside you, you are sitting in a straight and relaxed position and the first track of the *Transitioning* CD is playing.

2. As the CD slips onto the second track, allow yourself to return to the sacred space in which you found yourself in the previous exercise. This will be your home base from this point forward, the place from which each one of your writing efforts will begin.

3. While back in this space, allow yourself to relax into it. Use your deep exhales to dispel any tension from any source you may feel.

4. When you achieve a totally relaxed state you will feel a presence in your hands, a substance without determinable weight.

5. As you do, look down into your hands from your perspective in the image. What you will see or feel, if you are more kinesthetic than visual, is a

representation of a book, your book—the one which has been trying to get out of you.

6. In the image, turn it over, look at both covers, thumb through it if you would like, study the table of contents—whatever feels right to do.

7. After you have done exercise 6, open your eyes and write as fast as you can. Don't read what you write; just release and write whatever you are feeling at this moment.

Repeat this exercise as often as you would like to ask and get clarification on as much of the book as you feel you need to feel comfortable. Then move on to the next chapter. Remember, you can ask whatever questions of the DAW pertaining to this book or anything else before moving on.

> "Tis God gives skill, but not without men's hands.
> He could not make Antonio Stradivarius' violins
> without Antonio."
>
> —STRADIVARIUS

Chapter Ten

Write Your Publishable Book
In a Weekend Plan

I AM SURE YOU ARE CATCHING ON TO THE FACT THAT when it comes to writing a book, speed is not only good, but in most cases, absolutely necessary. The proper speed enables you to reach up and connect and then become one with the high vibrational content of your book. It is speed which also enables you to outrun Larry and all of the inhibitions and fears he carries along with him.

So, the closer you get to writing a book within three days (just because of logistics, I wouldn't recommend going much shorter), the better your results will be. Ultimately, both the experiential and qualitative results of your book will end up being better the faster you write your book. The shorter time it takes to write your book the better. This is why I eventually adjusted my retreat structure down to the three-day version.

If you are feeling intimidated by the concept of writing a book in three days right now, that may be normal. Remember that is why I wrote this book. It is designed to prepare you. If you have read this far and participated in the previous two exercises, you are ready to take the next step.

Change, no matter how good it may be at times, never feels comfortable. If you are feeling a bit of angst, anger, that I'm-out-of-here feeling right now, just understand that is normal. In fact, it is completely normal at this juncture. If you weren't feeling that way, to some level or another, there would be reason for concern.

You are at one of those times when you just need to walk through it, keep going, and hold to the old company line no matter what. As you continue to step forward, any anxiety will begin to dissipate and soon you will be running. Once there, Larry will no longer be able to keep up with you. By leaving him behind you will be leaving behind the fears he carries with him as well.

Before moving on to the reading of the following sections, pull out your regular-sized lined notebook and copy down any reminders you may need to derive from the information I provide below. Then keep those pages next to you while you are writing your book.

Initially they will serve as reminders of the guidelines you want to remember. Then they can serve as an aid in case your writing slows. In the case of your writing slowing down, not just over a fifteen-minute period but rather consistently, come back to your notes. See if you innocently veered outside the lines. If you did, get back in line by following the notes, and your speed will pick up and your book will begin to pour out of you again.

Constructing a Divine Physical Space

To be able to comfortably and thus successfully write a book in three days, it is important that you create a divine space in which to do so.

What do I mean by divine space?

- For some of you that will equate to a space in your own home, a room specifically set aside, with all of your favorite things around you, just for your writing.

- For the vast majority of you, a divine space will equate to leaving the responsibilities of your home space behind and relocating for three days to a hotel, beach house, cabin in the mountains, or retreat—a place that will allow you to devote your entire time to writing your book and the personal transformation that comes along with it.

Having this space in place will be absolutely essential

to the success of your efforts. Make sure to get it into place before embarking on this journey. Don't worry about leaving the comforts of home to find this space. That is normal.

A divine space that comes along with attending one of my Write Your Publishable Book in a Weekend retreats is a place for attendees to birth their books. They are simply there, in an uninterrupted space— away from the normal distractions of life and totally devoted to the birthing of their books. In every way, the intent behind the space is almost exact to the one we created for the birth of my daughter.

Everything was in place to welcome, in as glorious a manner as possible, this new soul into the world. You will be doing the same thing with the birthing of your book and your divine voice, message and self into the world as well. You need to either create a space or go to a provided space just like what it is available for retreat participants.

Leaving Your Cares Behind

Before entering into this divine space, it is essential that all of your responsibilities be covered for the time you will be writing your book. The last thing you want to be during this time is distracted by any outside influences.

So:

- Make sure anyone you are responsible to is informed about what you are doing. Don't expect all of them to be happy for you. Those who aren't consciously in connection with their DAWs will not understand your need to do what you are being drawn to do. Don't let their lack of enthusiasm for the step you are about to take discourage you.

"We can secure other people's approval, if we do right and try hard; but our own is worth a hundred of it..."

—MARK TWAIN

Allow your own enthusiasm for the step you are about to take fill in the gap you reserved for their affections. Life is all about learning to love ourselves, isn't it? Taking this step may just present you with an excellent opportunity to fine-tune your skills in this area.

- Make sure that the pets and plants are all taken care of. Even if you will be staying home, make sure that you have all the proper food in place for the pets; they may need a little extra attention during the time when you are turning your attention completely toward yourself. Talk to them as well. Tell them what you will be doing and ask for their cooperation. Pets understand much more than we realize. Since they have the ability to love unconditionally, they will be all about aiding you with your efforts however possible.

- Anticipate what could transpire over the five days you are writing and take care of all your responsibilities in advance. Will bills come due during that time? Pay them. Will your landscaper be coming by or a personal friend stopping by as usual on a certain day? Will they worry about you if you are not at home or interrupt you if you are? Take care of everything in advance.

"The ruling passion conquers reason still."

—ALEXANDER POPE

- Make sure that you have the proper food and refreshments with you and a good plan in place for how and when you will eat. Have plenty of high-protein snacks on hand. Writing a book can be like an athletic event where you need consistent nutrition.

- Stay away from the sugars and caffeine; they will get you up but also drop you flat on your face on the other side of the rise. Both sugars and caffeine also end up taking you to a place which constitutes the complete opposite of the place which is most convenient to meet your book, so stay away from them.

- That goes for drinks as well. Pure water is the best liquid to take into your system. Since writing your book will be taking you through an internal, physical transformation, it is important that you drink enough water each day to properly complete the flushing out of your system. That equates to approximately one ounce of water per two pounds of body weight. I use a forty-ounce water bottle to measure my intake every day, and end up drinking just over two of them daily to meet my needs.

- In regard to a meal schedule, either have your meals on hand, prepared, and tucked away in a refrigerator just waiting for you, or put a plan together to eat out at regular times during the day. However, if you are going to be eating out for lunch, make sure that doing so will not take you away from your writing for more than forty-five minutes. Doing so will just make it a lot harder to get reconnected to your DAW. In regard to your evening meal, if you have completed your quota of words for the day, which is 12,000 (an average of about 400 words per fifteen minutes x eight hours), take the evening off, unwind, and celebrate your efforts—remember the importance of positively reinforcing your writing efforts.

If you have not successfully completed your quota, show yourself great compassion. Don't be hard on yourself. Just simply have a short, nutritious meal that lasts no longer than forty-five minutes and then get back to it.

- Establish a specific writing and break schedule for yourself over your retreat. Starting as early as possible in the morning is best. Conclude late in the afternoon; try not to go into the evening, when your energy will drop. Your goal with your schedule is to write for eight good hours day—almost consecutively, with exception of your short breaks (forty-five minutes for lunch and two fifteen-minute breaks). It is just like a having a job, but hopefully one you like.

- A good writing hour equates to a minimum of at least 1,500 words an hour. Setting this schedule up in advance and committing to it is essential to your success. If you don't do so, too many opportunities will just be available for Larry to creep in and sabotage your efforts. If you have taken my advice to put together a contract to write your book and have distributed it to the five people I suggested, that will help immensely in curtailing Larry's ability to distract you as well.

What Else to Bring

- Draw a copy of the following list on your lined, regular-sized notebook. Put it on three consecutive pages. Fill a page out for each of the five days you will be working on your book.

Time I scheduled to meet with my DAW:

Time we actually met:

Our goal for today:

What we actually accomplished today:

Reinforcements I planned to offer myself for a job well done:

Reinforcements that I gave myself:

Other observations and notes:

My goal for my next session:

When we will meet again:

What I will use to reinforce my positive actions after the next session:

- My drawing pad (and a second one if I will be writing my book completely in longhand)

- My regular-sized, lined note book

- My little pad of paper

- Plenty of smooth-flowing pens

- My computer, if I am going to use one

- An external hard drive to routinely save my book

- An external keyboard if I would feel more comfortable with one

- Comfortable clothes

- Comfort things, like pillows

- Some sort of timing device, even if it is just a handheld watch, to time my writing output every fifteen minutes

- An iPod or device for listening to the *Transitioning* CD

- Snacks, food, and refreshments

Leading Up to Your Retreat

Make sure to:
- Complete your reading of this book

- Complete the previous writing exercises

- Have grown used to having the subliminal version of the *Transitioning* CD in the background throughout a good portion of the day

Once All of the Above Have Been Completed

- Pick a date to start

- Pick a place to hold your retreat

- Make all the proper arrangements

The Night Before Your Retreat

The night before you begin your personal retreat should be a sacred time, so that you can properly attune yourself to the revelation you are about to experience.If you find it necessary to bolster your confidence, visit my website and view a variety of the inspirational video testimonials.

I Am Thankful

"Gratitude is not only the greatest of virtues, but the parent of all the others."

—CICERO

1. Take some time to establish a quiet, sacred space for yourself. Try to do this before it is too late into the evening when you are tired and want to go to sleep.

2. Listen to and follow the instructions on the first track of the *Transitioning* CD, and then allow the CD to move on to the second track.

3. Once the second track starts to play, begin writing down as fast as possible the words "I am thankful for" followed by your response. Then repeat the exercise again and again— always writing as fast as possible—until you feel you have nothing else to say. This will prepare you to be in the necessary state of receptivity for beginning to write your book the next day.

Things to Keep in Mind during Your Personal Retreat

Don't Edit, Don't Read—Just Write

As mentioned, it is important to avoid, at all costs, reading, editing, or looking for mistakes when you are writing your book. There will be plenty of time for that later. Avoid doing anything with your book other than writing at this stage. Simply allow your DAW, no matter where it takes you, to express freely and openly. If Larry becomes obsessive and just keeps throwing out distraction after distraction, don't ignore him. That will only infuriate him further. Just keep writing as fast as you can and address any and all concerns he may toss at you by scribbling them down into your lined notebook. Doing so will give them an exit route out of your consciousness. That way they won't clog up your flow.

Post-Writing Research Gaps

My experience has shown me that an average of 98 percent of the material collected or studied during what I refer to as "pre-writing research" never ends up being used in the final draft of a book.

"A man will turn over half a library to make one

book."

—SAMUEL JOHNSON

If at all possible, I suggest you avoid, or severely limit, doing any pre-writing research. Just let the already completed book, which has been trapped inside you for maybe as long as decades, to come flowing out in its entirety.

> "If you steal from one author, it's plagiarism; if you steal from many, it's research."
>
> —WILSON MIZNER

During its release, if you come across a word that you can't recall or don't know how to spell, or if there is some fact, figure, or description you need to research, just leave a gap which you can come back to and fill in later during the revision stage that follows your ascent. Not only will this keep you from wasting valuable time by over-researching before the rough draft of the book is completed, this procedure will also keep you from interrupting the flow of your book as it is being released through you.

Keep the Flow Going: End in the Middle, Then Warm Up before Resuming

We are a people who possess a need for instant gratification. If we are dissatisfied with a movie, or a sporting event or a show on television, we immediately switch the channel. In regard to reading, fulfilling that desire for a sense of gratification or accomplishment translates to reading through to the end of a chapter or a section in a book before stopping.

However, when this tactic is applied to your DAW connection, it is completely counterproductive. When you conclude a connected session at the end of an expression, or a section or chapter, it makes it very difficult and sometimes impossible to reinvigorate the same energy and flow when reconnecting with your DAW for your next session.

To make it easiest for yourself to reconnect with where you were, how you felt, and what you were saying from a previous session, always finish your writing for the day in the midst of an expression. Then, all you will have to do in the next session to reconnect with the same exact flow is to enter into your DAW-connected state and recopy the last few words which you wrote most previously.

The result will not only make it easy to maintain your flow and momentum from session to session, but will also offer your DAW connection a seamlessness of expression.

Just Let the Words Fly

One of the keys to both releasing and maintaining your DAW connection comes from staying out of your Larry. Thus, when you are connected, just allow the words to fly out of you. This will enable you to stay within the necessary expressive speed of your DAW and ensure that you are remaining connected to it.

Writing as Fast as You Can

While I was with the Pirates, we once had a young player who was a great athlete but far from being one of the brightest persons on the planet. Shortly after we had called him up from the minor leagues and added him to our roster, he was installed as a mainstay at third base.

Defensively, third base, since it is so close to home plate, is a reactionary position. The ball comes at you so fast off the bat of a hitter that either you immediately know what to do with it or you're maimed for life.

This young player had grown up in a baseball family. In fact, his father had been a famous big leaguer. He was very familiar with the game, which helped him perform marvelously at his position.

However, it wasn't too long after he arrived, that the club decided to move him over to shortstop. Shortstop is commonly referred to as "the thinking man's position," because from there a player can control the entire infield. It is also approximately twice the distance from home plate as third base. So a player stationed at shortstop is often given much more time to ponder his or her move or reaction to a play.

This young player, as mentioned, was a phenomenal third baseman. However, he was a terrible defensive shortstop. After one game in which he had committed several errors, he was asked by a well-meaning reporter why it was that he was such a good third baseman yet not nearly as competent at his new position of shortstop.

A brighter player would have taken the question as an insult, but not this young player. He responded immediately without any bias or negative reaction at all. "Well ya know," he began, "when I was over at third base, you know, kinda like, when the ball was hit to me it got there real fast. But at shortstop, it bounces and bounces and bounces and takes a lot longer to get to me. In fact, it takes so long to get to me that I've got a lot of time to think about what it is that I am going to do with it when it finally gets there. And every time I think, I screw up."

"Every time I think, I screw up." How true, not only in baseball and with so much in life, but how especially appropriate with your writing.

> "God's gifts put man's best dreams to shame."
>
> —ELIZABETH BARRETT BROWNING

Thinking, of course, is a by-product of the Larry. Feeling is a by-product of your DAW connection. Thus, when writing effectively, it is in your best interest to always be feeling and not thinking.

The best way to avoid involving yourself with the latter is to write as fast as you can. When you write as fast as you can, you will stay within that DAW-connected state and there will be no room for "screwing up."

"In skating over thin ice our safety is in our speed."

—RALPH WALDO EMERSON

Writing as fast as you can cures another significant potential dilemma as well. Our emotions, understanding, interpretations, and reactions grow every day. As a result, in the course of a few years, our viewpoints on many major situations could change or alter substantially. These alterations in opinion and viewpoint will all be reflected in how your writing is expressed.

If you do not write fast and it takes you years to complete a book, you cannot help but have multiple potentially conflicting voices, viewpoints, and opinions coming through. Of course, this will not only be confusing for you at times but will also be especially perplexing for your readers. So, always just let the words flow and write as fast as you can.

How fast is fast enough? As mentioned previously, my experience has shown me that the slowest speed at which the DAW projects itself is approximately 1,200 words per hour. The average speed is around 1,500 words an hour. The highest consistent speed that I have ever seen sustained over a significant period of time is approximately 7,200 words an hour. By the way, the highest sustained writing speed I have ever seen at one of my retreats was over 4,800 an hour.

Remaining at as high a speed as possible maintains your necessary connection with your DAW, and ostracizes any and all forms of counterproductive intervention from Larry.

Reinforce, Reinforce, Reinforce, Rein...

So you don't forget to do so, lay out a list of potential reinforcements to offer yourself at the end of your writing session every day. As important as these reinforcements are, they need not be significant in monetary value to be effective.

Just make a list of all of the things you like to do for yourself each day and then choose as many of the activities or items off of the list for the day as you would like, if you make your goal.

With each reward you offer yourself say to yourself, "(enter your name here), this is for the good job you did with your writing today." This is referred to as *reparenting*. When this technique is applied, it won't take long before your Larry does an about-face and starts associating writing with receiving something good. When that happens he will lead you to the art form instead of away from it. It is then that things will really begin to happen for you. You will become positively addicted to your writing. When that happens, there will be no stopping you. You will treat your writing like an alcoholic treats a drink: you will just have to have it. The big difference between writing and alcoholism is that while alcoholics tear apart their lives and the lives of all those around them, the divine light energy that pours into you through your writing will do just the opposite. Hence why I refer to it as a "positive addiction."

Where to Conclude...

Make sure never to conclude a writing session at the end of a chapter or section. Doing so will just make jumping into your DAW during the next session too hard—at times impossible. So, instead, always conclude a writing session in the midst of a chapter or section in your book.

How to Warm Up

Warm up at the beginning of each writing session by recopying the last twenty to thirty words you wrote during your most recent session. Doing so will blend you right back into the flow where you left off the time before.

To Read or Not to Read

Outside of required reading for your job or profession, and magazines and newspapers, don't do any reading while completing your book. After you have found, acknowledged, and embraced your voice, you can go back to reading whatever you want. Remember not to do so before the completion of your first book using this method.

Going Where?

It is important to keep in mind that no matter how much preparatory work we have done up until this point, you'll still not know where you are going with your writing from day to day. This is your DAW's way of keeping you interested, so don't expect anything more. Just sit back, enjoy the ride, and let the book take you on the journey of a lifetime.

> "I am in earnest; I will not equivocate; I will not excuse; I will not retreat a single inch; and I will be heard!"
>
> —WILLIAM LLOYD GARRISON

Slow Then Fast

The writing of any major project usually starts off slowly for the first few hours to potentially early into the second day. In fact, it is not unusual for some switching back and forth by your DAW in regard to the point of view employed—whether the first or third person is used. You may even find that the book you thought you were writing completely changes venues leading into the second day. This is not unusual, and with writing, nothing is ever wasted.

Even that writing which does not end up in the

final draft of the book has served a valuable purpose by either preparing you to write your book or removing some emotional resistance that may have been keeping you from taking that step. Until you both get used to each other, don't allow any early sluggishness to rattle you. It will all smooth out faster than you think. Just keep this in mind and stay within the routine. In no time your book will have adjusted to you and you to it. When that happens, you both will begin operating as one, and everything will go a lot smoother.

Nap Time

Whenever Thomas Edison used to run into a problem with one of his inventions, he used to take a catnap. That's right: he used to allow himself to take a catnap. You see, Edison believed that when one slept, his or her soul left the body and went to a higher level of consciousness. Then it came back and re-entered the body upon reawakening, bringing back with it whatever information it was lacking or needed to know.

You may find Edison's theory helpful with your writing. You may even find yourself starting to fall asleep during your writing sessions. This is not because your writing is boring. This is happening because your DAW is reaching for a higher level of understanding it wants to bring into your writing, which it can't quite reach while you are in a waking state. So, if you feel as though you want to go to sleep during a writing session, allow yourself to do so. Just put your head down on your desk and nod off. In no time at all, you will wake back up with a renewed vigor and point of view that wasn't there before falling asleep.

The Final Five

To help ease Larry's concerns about where the hell you're going and what you're doing, you may want to use the last five minutes of each writing session to jot down where your DAW has shown you you're going in the next session. That way, with a road map of at least the next day's destination squarely in front of it, your Larry won't feel so lost and out of control.

The Last Ten

You may also want to reserve the last ten minutes or so before you retire for the evening to do some brainstorming on paper. Doing so especially helps to prime your consciousness for really taking off with your DAW the next morning. After arising, if you experience any sluggishness at all with your writing, you will find that doing this usually cures it instantly.

The Real Poop

Since the side of us that we tap into when writing affects us personally, it is not unusual for a person to experience a short period of time when the poop in other areas of his or her life seems to be hitting the fan. If that begins to happen to you, don't overreact.

Everything and everyone will calm down in a few days as they adjust to the massive amount of new energy you're allowing through your writing. Everything will be okay as long as you don't overreact and you just let things settle on their own. Believe me, I know.

> "Beyond plants are animals, beyond animals is man, beyond man is the universe, the Big Light, let the Big Light in!"
>
> —JEAN TOOMER

All On Its Own

Like that personal or professional relationship that had already expired and was just hanging on, you will just know when the book has ended. Plus, you will literally not be able to write anything more on the book that hasn't already been written.

> "If we weren't all crazy, we would go insane."
>
> —JIMMY BUFFETT

The book will just end on its own and it won't give you any more than a few minutes notice, if that, before doing so. That way, Larry won't be able to screw up the ending, which he is famous for doing.

> "If you limit your choices only to what seems possible or reasonable, you disconnect yourself from what you truly want, and all that is left is a compromise."

—ROBERT FRITZ

Then What?

We'll get into that at the end of the book. For now, just concentrate on getting ready to birth your book.

The Last Words

Remember that all you need to know you already know, and all you need to have you already have in your possession. To remind yourself of this fact, all you have to do is look back through this book at everything you have already learned.

"Inspiration is the act of drawing up a chair to the writing desk."

—ANONYMOUS

CHAPTER ELEVEN

GO

"Do or do not. There is no try."

—YODA

O KAY, IT'S TIME TO BEGIN. I WILL GET YOU STARTED, but from this point forward it will be you and your DAW writing your project through your Ruby.

"He is not busy being born; he is busy dying."

—BOB DYLAN

Step 1: Flip on the first track of your *Transitioning* CD and follow the routine steps to get into your DAW-connected state.

Step 2: Once the CD moves into the second track, open up to a blank page in your large drawing pad. In the center write the words, "I am ready to begin the writing of my book."

> "There is the risk you cannot afford to take [and] there is the risk you cannot afford not to take."
>
> —PETER DRUCKER

Step 3: Allow yourself to completely associate freely with any thoughts or feelings, whether they are directly tied to what you will be writing or not, by releasing them onto the lineless piece of paper before you. Make sure to circle each expression and then connect each circled item to the nearest item to it with a straight line. The consistent use of circles, since they have no beginning and no end, will confuse linear Larry, who will then let down his guard and allow the info listed in the circles to transfer over to Ruby, through whom your DAW will then be given the chance to speak. As with all your writing, remember to allow this expression to fly out of you as fast as you can.

"Man came forth from God and must return to God."

—BAIRD T. SPALDING

Life and Teaching of the Masters
of The Far East

Step 4: The process will start off in a staccato fashion, with one- or two-word expressions initially being shot out of you. As your consciousness is switched over to Ruby and your DAW, the master of flow, your writing will begin to lengthen into phrases, sentences, and then paragraphs if you stay with it. However, before your writing turns into paragraphs, open up to a blank page in your drawing pad and start to write linearly. Keep in mind all that we have gone over up to this point, especially about writing as fast as you can, not reading or judging your material, and always writing what you feel. Stay with this until your first break, which should be in about two hours. Then break for fifteen minutes. Come back and recopy your last twenty to thirty words. With the subliminal track of the CD playing in the background, pick up where you left off and keep going. Two hours later, take a lunch or meal break of no longer than forty-five minutes. Then come back, prime your writing pump by going through the first track of the CD. Then when the CD moves on to its second track, recopy the last twenty to thirty words you wrote before your meal and continue writing. Then break again in another two hours for fifteen minutes. Flow back into your material in the same manner you did for the first break in the day. After another two hours of writing, you are done for the day if you have reached your quota of 12,000 words. If not, take a fifteen minute break and come back for another session long enough to take you to your quota. Minus the circle drawing, follow this same sequence of events each day of the scheduled three days, or however long it takes you to complete your book.

"In the depth of winter, I finally learned that within me there lay an invincible summer."

—ALBERT CAMUS

Chapter Twelve

Revision and Completion

YOU HAVE FINISHED WRITING YOUR BOOK. Congratulations!

"The artist is nothing without the gift, but the gift is nothing without work."

—EMILE ZOLA

If you have followed the aforementioned steps to a tee, 85 percent of the work necessary to fully complete your book is now done. The most important thing to keep in mind is that, even though we may be way ahead on the scorecard, the war has not been won yet. There is still important work that needs to be done.

The most sage advice that I can offer you at this stage of your development is to:

1. keep your momentum, which you have worked so hard to acquire, rolling right into the revision of your book

2. e-mail me at TomBird@TomBird.com to inform me that you have completed the writing of your book and to get the link to download the *Revision* CD that will set the stage for you, much in the same manner that *Transitioning* did for you and your writing, to successfully complete the revision of your book, and

3. use the *Revision* CD in the exact same manner that you did *Transitioning* to get to this stage. Do so by simply working your way through the first track of the CD to prepare you to revise and then use the subliminal side to keep you in that state as you revise.

The Revision Begins—The First Sweep-Through

Step 1: Repeat this phase until you have completely fulfilled the objective of this exercise. Always start by using your new CD to enter into your DAW-connected state.

Step 2: Read through your book, noting any and all major changes or alterations you would like to make to your work.

If you have written the majority or all of your book in longhand, Post-it notes of varying colors work especially well with this phase. Just color code the type of changes you want to make, jot down on a Post-it what change is meant to happen and slap it on the paper where it is supposed to go.

If using your computer, a similar procedure can be developed through Word. Major changes are defined as any alterations, rearrangements, subtractions, or additions that directly affect the general theme or direction of what you have already written. This does not include grammatical changes and/or the correction of typographical mistakes.

Step 3: Despite how many sessions it takes, do not move on to the next step until you have fully completed this one. Remember, what worked so well with your writing also will work with your revision. So the quicker you can move through this step, the better.

Making Those Changes

Step 1: Using your *Revision* CD, enter into your DAW-connected state.

Step 2: At this stage, always moving from the front of your book to the back, make whatever general changes you have proposed for your book.

If you wrote your book on paper, you may have to use several other pieces of your chosen writing surface to do so. It may take several days to complete this task.

In that case, simply follow these two steps each time you go into your manuscript to make the necessary changes, rearrangements, or additions. Don't move on to the next step until you have fully completed this one.

Post-Writing Research

After you have completed any and all necessary changes to your project, use the *Revision* CD to get into your DAW-connected state. Then go back through your manuscript and fill in all the informational and expressional gaps.

Remember the value of speed. The faster you move the less time you have to "think." Where there is a lack of time to think there is also a lack of Larry, who would still like to screw up things.

> "I dare not alter these things; they come to me from above."
>
> —ALFRED AUSTIN

At This Point

At this point, structually, you have done everything you can possibly do to your book. If publication is the goal, it is now time to turn your book over to seasoned professionals, meaning a style and eventually a copy editor.

Chapter Thirteen

Acknowledging the New You

Your book is now done, and it is time to access exactly how you have changed and grown. It is very important that you do this so you can consciously accept these enlightenments into the very fiber of your life.

What I Have Discovered about Myself

> "An author arrives at a good style when his language performs what is required of it without shyness."
>
> —CYRIL CONNOLLY

1. Use your *Transitioning* CD to enter into your DAW-connected state, which you should be so familiar with by now.

2. Once you have moved beyond the first track and into the second track of the CD, ask yourself the question, "What have I discovered about myself, my life, and those around me through the process of writing my book?" Then allow your response to that question to flow onto your large drawing pad.

"The proper study of mankind is books."

—ALDOUS HUXLEY

Chapter Fourteen

Publication and Beyond

"You can convert your style into riches..."

—QUENTIN CRISP

Publishing Your Book

PERSONALLY, I WAS NEVER OF THE OPINION THAT publication of one's book, because of all the other benefits associated with writing, was essential to being coined a successful author. Of course, that was a few decades ago. Today I feel that it is absolutely essential to publish one's work. Not only have times changed so drastically and for the better in the literary world, but the evolution of our day and time seems to support the notion that many voices can be heard.

> "If wisdom were offered me with this proviso that I should keep it close and not communicate it, I would refuse the gift. There is no delight in owning anything unshared."
>
> —SENECA

For detailed information on publishing and all that goes with it, please either check out my book *Write to Publish* or the information on my Publish Now Program, which can be found at *www.publishnow.com*.

> "When you cease to make a contribution, you begin to die."
>
> —ELEANOR ROOSEVELT

Beyond

> "I came to the conclusion that one of the reasons why I'm so blessed, I think, is because I reach so many people, and you never know whose life you are touching or affecting. And so, because your blessings come back to you based upon how you give them out...that's why I'm so...You know what I'm saying? You get it? Okay, good."
>
> —OPRAH WINFREY

From the process you have just gone through, you have learned, grown, and released much, and for that I congratulate you. As I mentioned, everyone I have ever gotten to know has been drawn at one time or another to write a book, yet so few have had the drive to do so. That makes you one of the brave, the elite. Hopefully, those around you have been open enough on their own to your accomplishments to have grown and fed off your efforts as well.

As the result of what you have done, you have learned not only how to write a book but you have become an author; there is no reason to stop there. If you are like those wonderful souls whose presence I have been so blessed by in my own life—those who have attended my workshops and classes—what you have accomplished equates to just a start for you. There are other books and dreams inside you just waiting to emerge and live.

In regard to writing the other books, simply follow the steps in the chapters on composing your books, and let them flow out of you. My book on publishing is also an excellent guide in quickly, easily, cheaply and very profitably getting your work not only published but distributed worldwide.

Regarding your other dreams and aspirations, no matter how varied they may be, writing can help you there as well. When you write through the divine method which was given to me and which was my pleasure to share with you, you connect directly with God. Whether God lives in you or outside of you doesn't matter. You can now directly reach him/her, and he/she can reach you.

> "God does not exist apart from you. God is the essence of your being. God dwells within your heart and within the hearts of all beings."
>
> —PAUL FERRINI
>
> *Return to the Garden*

In my view, this is the greatest gift bestowed by writing. Use this gift to go beyond writing to wherever it is you want go, no matter what it is you want to do. Make that connection—you know how to do it. You have done it, and you still retain those tools. Ask questions and receive divine responses. Seek direction and receive it. Live your abilities to their fullest potential. Be the example you were born to be.

> "The most important thing is to be whatever you are without shame."
>
> —ROD STEIGER

The "Force" is now with you. It is you. You don't have to go through anyone or anything else to access it. Use it wisely, but use it as it was meant to be used, as it wants to be used, as you need to use it. It is here for you and you are here for it —the perfect partnership. And now, right now, is that time to birth it. It seeks to be birthed, for you to birth it directly into your life and all the lives that you touch—with every breath and heartbeat; every minute, hour, day, month, and year; every book.

Your world has been returned to you; it once again belongs to you. Do with it as you choose. Whether you do it for yourself, for others, or for both, just live. No matter what you do, live. This is exactly what you were born to do.

"This above all: To thine own self be true."

—SHAKESPEARE

Made in the USA
Middletown, DE
18 June 2015